LORD, I'VE GOT A PROBLEM

DON BAKER

HARVEST HOUSE PUBLISHERS
Eugene, Oregon 97402

To the First Evangelical Free Church
family of Rockford, Illinois

LORD, I'VE GOT A PROBLEM

Copyright © 1988 by Harvest House Publishers
Eugene, Oregon 97402

Library of Congress Catalog Card Number 87-082258
ISBN 0-89081-638-7

Printed in the United States of America.

Contents

"Problems, Problems, Problems"
❦

Don't read this book if you're convinced that Christians are not supposed to have problems.

Everyone has problems, even Christians.

I have problems. And I can identify with almost every problem described in this book.

I am anxiety prone.

I have been hospitalized with depression.

I have suffered a stroke, polio, and cancer.

I have watched a son die.

I have been tempted.

I know the pain of guilt.

I know the awesome power of fear.

I've known the loneliness of leadership.

I've experienced anger from both friends and enemies. I've been angry and I know the terrible distance it creates between people.

I'm aging. I once thought that problems would diminish with age. They do not. In fact, problems seem to increase with age.

Jesus promised us problems. He said:
> "In the world you have tribulation [problems], but take courage; I have overcome the world" (John 16:33).

In Jesus, we are not free from problems, but we have resources with which to overcome them.

The following chapters will point you to God's resources for dealing with the problems we all face. I hope you will find God's resources as helpful as I have.

Loneliness

What is loneliness?

What causes loneliness?

Is there a cure for loneliness?

*Is there more to loneliness
than just being alone?*

Where can intimacy be found?

How can intimacy be experienced?

Lord, I've got a problem.
I'm so lonely it hurts.
I'm seldom alone,
but still feel lonely. 🍎

Adam and Eve had something special in Eden.
   Clothed only with the ethereal light of God's
glory, they knew nothing of
      fear
         guilt
            shyness
               or shame.
   They lived in a paradise which sprang from the
creative genius of the Architect of the universe.
They spent every evening with Him.

Each day God would come calling.
Adam wasn't worried about the lawn.
Eve wasn't concerned about the china.
They felt no need to impress, no pressure to prepare.
Each day was lived in anticipation of God's visit.

Each afternoon as the shadows lengthened, the first human beings would wait hand in hand for the sounds of their Friend as He approached.
They would greet Him warmly and then relax to chat about the adventures of exploring the joys of a new creation.
Each night was filled with pleasant memories.

Then they "blew it."
One evening as the sun lowered itself in the western sky and the earth was quietly relaxed waiting for darkness to fall, God came.
He knocked. No one answered.
He searched. No one appeared.
He called. No one responded.

Finally, a man and a woman slowly emerged from behind the shrubs. Their heads were lowered. Their eyes were downcast. The light that had surrounded them had disappeared.
Fig leaves covered their nakedness. They were ashamed.
They had hid. They were afraid.
The early evening visits ended.
The friendly chats stopped.
The friendship terminated.
God and His first couple were separated.

The creature was separated from his Creator.

In their separation from God, Adam and Eve were the first to experience loneliness.

Adam and Eve slid into the loneliness of their guilt.

God withdrew into the loneliness of man's rejection.

Loneliness is the curse of separation.

Separation is the result of sin.

Loneliness is a feeling of isolation, of standing apart from others. It's a feeling of emptiness, a feeling of loss. It's a craving for intimacy.

Nearly 50 million Americans have been stricken with what some call a new nationwide epidemic of loneliness.

John Gunther refers to it as one of the supreme American problems.

What causes loneliness?

Separation is the root cause.

Adam and Eve were created to enjoy, and to be enjoyed by, God. That relationship became clouded by their act of disobedience.

Sin gave birth to such feelings as
  envy
    jealousy
      rivalry
        hostility
          rejection
          and hatred.

Intimacy was lost. Fellowship was destroyed. A social clumsiness was admitted into human relationships that was never known in those wonderful early days of Eden.

Death causes loneliness.

I spotted a widow sitting alone in a restaurant. She had recently lost her husband. I greeted her. Without saying hello, she looked up at me and pointed across the table to the opposite chair. "That's where John always sat," she said.

Divorce causes loneliness.

The first year after a disabling divorce is a time of intense loneliness.

Urbanization causes loneliness.

Condominiums, high-rise apartments, town houses, government subsidized housing, and much of our urban lifestyle causes alienation and loneliness.

Moving causes loneliness.

One in every five Americans moves each year. This lack of roots and lasting relational ties is responsible for much loneliness.

Fear causes loneliness.

Once I attempted to help an elderly woman as she struggled through the rain with a heavy load of groceries. As I approached her, she screamed, dropped her groceries and ran for the nearest house. I never could convince her that I only wanted to help her.

Age causes loneliness.

A child is lonely when he has no one to play with.

A youth is lonely when his peers reject him.

An adult is lonely when he has no one with whom to share dreams and joys.

An elderly person is lonely when he no longer feels needed.

A 90-year-old retired businessman sat in his small room in a nursing home. His head rested on his little bedside table.

After our initial greeting, I asked him what he was doing.

He looked at me and said, "I'm just waiting."

"Waiting for what," I asked.

"Oh, just waiting," he answered. "Waiting to go to the bathroom and waiting to die."

One's world gets quite lonely when it gets that small.

Is there a cure for loneliness?

Yes. Here are some guidelines for combatting loneliness.

Re-establish fellowship with God.

Jesus Christ has bridged the chasm of separation in order to bring God and man together again. He is called the Reconciler.

The wedge of distance can only be removed when we acknowledge that sin is the culprit and that Jesus is the remedy.

The only way to get back into the "family" and to enjoy undisturbed oneness is by receiving Jesus, God's Son.

> "But as many as received Him, to them He gave the right to become children of God, even to those who believe in His name" (John 1:12).

Re-examine relationships with people.

A poor self-image, anger, hostility, selfishness, even body odor or bad breath can injure relationships.

Friendships are damaged when we enter them with a goal to get rather than to give.

Loneliness is often the cause of personality quirks that repel people like flea powder repels fleas. One of the biggest steps a lonely person can take is to ask a trusted friend or counselor the question, "Why don't people want to be around me?"

Our friends usually know, and if they are truly our friends they will tell us.

Is there more to loneliness than just being alone?

It appears that being alone is seldom the problem.

We all need solitude occasionally.

Solitude and loneliness are not the same.

Loneliness is more a problem of insulation

than isolation. Lonely people may spend their lives with others. They may be like Albert Einstein, who said, "It is strange to be known so universally, and yet be so lonely."

Tim Timmons, one of my favorite authors, is a wonderfully able and popular speaker. He is gregarious, personable and approachable. In his book on loneliness, however, he describes himself as a person who once was painfully lonely. He didn't recognize his inner pain as loneliness. He blamed his anxious feelings on such things as depression, anger, guilt, or even a headache.

He was finally able to identify his problem when he was confronted with the word "intimacy."

Intimacy is more than just having people around us.

Intimacy requires a relationship that moves beyond the surface to become deep and meaningful.

An intimate relationship is one that removes masks and lifts veils.

Intimacy cares and dares.

An intimate person is willing to make himself known and to search out and know another in return.

Intimacy is terribly threatening to most of us. In becoming intimate
   I open myself to another
      I make myself vulnerable
         I stop pretending.
I share my humanness and, in return, I receive the humanness of another.

Together we then give our humanness to God.

Jesus modeled intimacy for us. He allowed Himself to be known. He kept no secrets.

When asked where He lived, Jesus didn't just give an address or directions. He said, "Come and see."

We all crave a meaningful relationship—the kind that is able to discuss something other than
>food
>>jobs
>>>cars
>>>>and money.

We crave relationships which welcome talk about
>feelings
>>failures
>>>and fears.

We crave relationships that are willing to
>bear burdens
>>confess faults
>>>and encourage one another.

We crave relationships that believe there is something very sacred and very powerful about the gathering of two or three people with Jesus present.

We crave relationships that move beyond companionship to compassion.

We crave relationships that are as interested in "being" as in "doing."

What we all want is a relationship that will permit "being" without "pretending."

We want a relationship that will allow us to speak without needing to choose our words.

We want a relationship that will even permit
silence without suspicion.

That's intimacy.

Where can intimacy be found?

Intimacy was originally found in the Garden of
Eden.

Calvary is where intimacy was regained.

Jesus died to eliminate separation.

"We were reconciled to God through
the death of His Son" (Romans 5:10).

Jesus lives to create intimacy.

"He Himself has said, 'I will never de-
sert you, nor will I ever forsake you' "
(Hebrews 13:5).

The Church is the agency Jesus established to
meet the needs of a world filled with lonely
people.

The Church is where intimacy is to be enjoyed.

The Church is God's provision for our need for
caring and warmth and mutual self-disclosure.

The Church is designed to provide us with
experiences of honesty and openness and
protection.

The Church is where two, four, six, eight, or
more people actually become one.

The Christians described in Acts 2 comprised
just that kind of church. Each day they met to gain
strength from their Lord and from each other, and
each day they went out energized to transform
their world.

You didn't know there were churches like that?

There *are* churches like that—and more are coming into existence all over the world. It's hard to find them among the affluent and self-contained churches. But where there is need and pain and loneliness, there is usually a church with intimacy.

How can one experience intimacy?

Look for an intimate church.

Look until you find one.

Find a community of Christians that places higher priority on people than on programs.

Find a church that is more concerned about building lives than building buildings.

Find a church that is more anxious to help its community than to impress it.

Find a church that desires to please God rather than man.

When you find that church, move into it and become part of it in spite of the apprehension you may feel. Attach yourself to a small group of caring people. Learn to
> share with them
> care with them
> pray with them
> and grow with them.

Learn to listen.

Intimacy demands attentiveness.

Attentiveness requires more than hearing what is said. It requires hearing what is meant and what is felt.

It requires that I listen with more than my ears. I also listen with my eyes in an attempt to see beyond the surface. I listen with my heart to hear what's taking place down deep in another's soul.

Jesus reminded us that it is possible to have eyes and not see, and to have ears and not hear.

Intimacy demands that I know when another is hurting even when he can't tell me verbally.

Intimacy requires the efforts of at least two people.

Learn to be honest.

I was stunned one day when I casually asked a stranger, "How are you?"

She stopped, looked at me and said, "Please don't ask me that question unless you really want to know."

We really don't want to know who is hurting and why, and we don't want others to know when we hurt. Intimacy can never be experienced in the presence of dishonesty.

Jesus modeled this kind of honesty when He told His disciples:

"My soul is deeply grieved to the point of death" (Mark 14:34).

Then He asked them to pray for Him.

Intimacy risks the sharing of feelings. Intimacy speaks the truth in love. Intimacy is honest—not cruel, not blunt, but honest.

Learn to guard confidences.

Most people have ceased being honest because their honest feelings and their honest secrets, shared in confidence, have been shared with others.

Learn to be available.

Intimacy costs something. We must learn to be available to others—even at inconvenient times.

Obstetricians learn to be available to babies who want to be born in the middle of the night.

Pastors learn to handle crises which occur late on Saturday night.

Responding to people's crises, even at inconvenient times, builds relationships.

Learn to pray.

When Jesus asked His disciples to pray for Him, He was modeling intimacy.

When I pray for another, I become a vital part of that person's being and life. It bonds us as nothing else can.

We all need to belong to a community of caring Christians. I have watched numerous small groups of caring Christians move from fear and suspicion to intimacy.

A young husband was involved in a shattering automobile accident. By the time I arrived at the hospital, three couples were already there surrounding his frightened wife.

By the time the doctor came with the news that he was unable to save the man's life, three more couples had arrived. They immersed the grieving widow in their caring and strengthened her.

That's intimacy. That's God's provision for loneliness.

That sort of giving and receiving not only transforms individual lives, it transforms churches and makes them irresistible to the communities around them.

If no such community of caring Christians is available in your area, create one. All it takes is two people who love Jesus and are willing to let Jesus show them how to love others.

And then watch your loneliness disappear.

For Further Reading

Terry Hershey. *Intimacy—The Longing of Every Human Heart.* Eugene, OR: Harvest House Publishers, 1988.

Bruce Larson. *There's a Lot More to Health Than Not Being Sick.* Waco, TX: Word Books.

Carin Rubenstein and Phillip Shaver. *In Search of Intimacy.* New York: Delacorte Press, 1982.

Tim Timmons. *Loneliness Is Not a Disease.* Eugene, OR: Harvest House Publishers, 1981.

Fear

How common is the problem of fear?
What does fear feel like?
Is fear solely a spiritual problem?
How can a person be relieved of fear?

Lord, I've got a problem.
I'm afraid. 🍎

Fear does strange things to people—to good people, even godly people.

Abraham was a godly person who did a strange thing—a very strange thing. Because he was afraid, he gave his wife to another man.

Sarah was a godly woman who did a strange thing—a very strange thing. Because she was afraid, she gave her husband to another woman.

To give away one's mate to another is a strange thing—a very strange thing—in any age, in any culture, for any reason. But it's unthinkable that

people of faith would give away their mates
because of fear.

But let me tell you the story.

It happened in ancient Egypt.

Abraham and Sarah were tourists in Egypt
waiting for the crops to grow again in Canaan.

Egypt was ruled by a king called a pharaoh.
The pharaohs were gods to the people of the Nile.
A pharaoh could
   say anything he wished
    do anything he wished
     have anything he wished.
A pharaoh could have another man's
  land
   or tents
    or wealth
     or life
      or even his wife
      if he wished.

Abraham was afraid that the pharaoh would
want his wife. He said to Sarah:
    "You are a beautiful woman. . . .
    When the Egyptians see you, . . . they
    will kill me. . . . Please say that you
    are my sister so that it may go well
    with me" (Genesis 12:11-13).
She did. Sarah told all who met them that she
was Abraham's sister, not his wife.

They did. The Egyptians saw Sarah and they
praised her beauty.

He did. Pharaoh heard about the beautiful
stranger from Canaan and wanted her for his wife.

Abraham was treated well as Sarah's "brother." The grateful pharaoh gave him

sheep
and oxen
and donkeys
and camels
and servants.

Pharaoh was not treated well by God, however. An angry God struck him with a plague.

The plague continued until the frightened pharaoh returned Sarah to her husband.

Most men would die for their wives. Abraham gave his away.

Fear does strange things to people, doesn't it?

Sarah was not only beautiful, she was also godly.

But she was afraid. God had promised that her children would someday rule the earth.

Her problem? She had no children. And at age 76, with an 86-year-old man for a husband, she didn't have much hope of ever bearing a child.

What did she do? She gave her husband Abraham to another woman who could bear a child for her.

Because of his fear, Abraham gave his wife to another man.

Because of her fear, Sarah gave her husband to another woman.

Abraham's fear focused on death—he didn't want to die.

Sarah's fear also focused on death—she didn't want to die without a son.

Fear does strange things to people, doesn't it?

Fear still does strange things to people, even
godly people.
Fear can keep us from
  riding in elevators
    flying in airplanes
      making a decision
        sharing an experience
          getting married
            having children
              teaching a class
                meeting a stranger
                  even answering the phone.
Fear can cause us to focus all our energies on
  aging
    illness
      disaster
      dying
        nuclear weapons
          failure
            or rejection.
A young woman I know is so afraid of
rejection that she cannot speak to men.

Fear hurts.
Its gnawing pain can invade every part of a
person's being.
Many have asked me, "Are you ever afraid
when you stand up to speak?"
"Always," I answer.
And those fears cause tremors in my hands,
shaking in my knees, tension in my voice, sickness

in my stomach, perspiration on my forehead, tightness in my chest, and stiffness in my neck.

Those fears cause shortness in my temper, quickness in my step, and the almost overwhelming urge to run and hide and never return.

Fear is common.
Fear *is* disabling.
Fear can
  shorten life
    destroy relationships
      create emotional problems
       cause spiritual crises
        make one's whole life
miserable.

I read a startling statement recently. It said that fear is not a psychological problem, but an educational problem.

I immediately rejected it—until I thought about it.

I shared the statement with a friend who has been grappling with an obsessive fear for years.

She immediately rejected it—until she thought about it.

Fear *is* an educational problem.
Fear is related to something I know or don't know.

Abraham didn't know his new God well enough.

He knew his old gods. He knew that the old gods of Mesopotamia could make promises but couldn't keep them.

Abraham needed to learn something. He needed to learn that his new God, Jehovah, never made a promise He wouldn't keep, and that He never broke any promise He made.

Abraham didn't believe that God could preserve him in a pagan culture.

Sarah didn't believe that God could give a son to an old woman.

They both needed to learn something about God.

And learn they did. Abraham's fear eventually diminished to the point that he was willing to slay the son that God had promised him.

If God wanted his son sacrificed, Abraham would do it and believe that God would then bring that son back from the dead.

How were Abraham and Sarah's fears relieved?

How were their fears replaced by a serene and strong faith?

Relieving fear is a two-step process. It's like walking. One step gets you nowhere. It takes two steps to get somewhere.

The first step is to learn something.

It's an intellectual step. It's mental.

For Abraham, learning involved a promise God had made to him.

While still in ancient Ur, Abraham heard some words from God that only faith could grasp.

God told Abraham that He would
  give him land
  make him the father
  of a great nation
  bless him
  make his name great
  and bless all the families
  of the earth through him.

The only thing Abraham had to do was to
leave Ur, leave his home, leave his family, leave his
friends and travel a thousand miles with
  his wife
  his nephew
  his tents
  his sheep
  his cattle
  his donkeys
  his oxen
  and his servants
  on foot!
There were
  no moving vans
  no trains
  no planes
  no cars
  not even a U-Haul trailer.
Abraham was asked to travel a thousand miles
on the strength of only one promise.

He heard the promise, filtered it through his
brain, memorized it, meditated on it, and weighed
its consequences.

Fear

He evaluated the God who had made the promise, studied all the maps that were available, checked with his travel agent, conferred with his wife, and talked with his parents.

Then Abraham was ready for the second step.

The second step is to do something.

It's a responsive step. It requires action.
"So Abram went forth as the LORD
had spoken to him" (Genesis 12:4).

It made no difference that Abraham was 75 years old. He went anyway.

Action is based on information.

Abraham learned the promise, then acted on it.

Both steps are required to relieve fear.

When Abraham displayed his fears in Egypt, and when Sarah displayed her fears in Canaan, their faith was young, untried and inexperienced.

They were just getting to know God.

The more they learned of Him, and the more they acted upon what they knew, the less fear they experienced.

Flying can be a frightening experience—even to those who fly frequently.

When I was in college I took flight training.

Flight training involved two steps—ground school and flight school. In ground school we learned the theory of flight. And in flight school we put theory into practice.

Ground school relieved the fear of flying. Flight school removed it.

Fear is relieved by learning all we can about the thing we fear. Then, on the strength of what we know, fear is removed by action.

Let's learn some things about fear.

Fear does not come from God.

When I am afraid, I need to remember that my fear does not come from God:

> "For God has not given us a spirit of
> timidity [fear], but of power and love
> and discipline" (2 Timothy 1:7).

Fear has its root in sin, not in God. Adam was the first person to experience fear, the first to experience its power, the first to speak its name.

"I was afraid," he said as he heard God approaching after he had committed the first act of sin.

Fear has its source in Satan. If God has not given us the spirit of fear, then fear becomes suspect. Fear may be caught and it may be taught. But most often fear comes from the enemy and he paralyzes us with its presence.

Fear is an illusion.

It comes from impaired judgment, from a mind out of focus. Fear is often grounded in
something in the past
that didn't happen
or something in the future
that hasn't happened
and likely won't ever happen.
My wife and I drove across the country recently—in two cars—moving from Illinois to

Oregon. We each wore a voice-actuated headset which allowed us to communicate as we drove.

While I was traveling at 65 miles per hour, a large metal garbage barrel fell from a truck directly in front of me. I braked, swerved and missed the barrel, and shouted a warning into the headset. My wife, who was two cars behind me and unable to see the problem, braked at my warning, swerved and only slightly tapped the barrel with her bumper.

In that moment of stress there was no fear—just competent, decisive, evasive action. And as a result, no accident occurred.

The fear came later—not over what happened, but over what could have happened.

Fear after the fact is common, and it's human. But we must admit that it is sort of stupid to fear something that didn't happen. Fearing what might have happened is unnecessary.

Love is God's provision for fear.

It's at this point that you might be tempted to put the book down or throw it away.

Please don't!

The most important thing to learn about fear is to learn what God has provided to overcome it.

"There is no fear in love; but perfect love casts out fear" (1 John 4:18).

We usually think that the opposite of fear is faith and the opposite of love is hate. John tells us that the opposite of fear is love. Love casts out fear.

Do you remember the story about the little blind girl who was seated with her daddy on the front porch of her home?

A friend came by the house. Knowing that the girl could not see, the friend decided to play a trick on her. He walked quietly up the steps and, without a word, grabbed her from her father's arms and then, running, carried her down the street.

The girl didn't make a sound. She didn't try to break free. She relaxed in those strange arms.

The friend stopped, put her down and identified himself.

"Weren't you afraid?" he asked.

"No," she replied.

"Did you know who I was?"

"No, I didn't know who you were."

"Since you couldn't see me and didn't know who I was, why were you willing to let me run away with you?"

"I didn't need to see you," she answered. "My daddy could see you and he knew who you were. Since you didn't frighten him, I knew everything was all right."

When I am finally able to accept my Father's perfect love for me, then my fears can relax. I know that He will not allow anything to enter my life without first giving it permission. And I know that He will not permit anything to enter my life without also providing His presence.

That's the promise of love.

Move ahead in spite of fear.

Knowing these things about fear, the next step is to move ahead anyway. Knowing is only the first step. Doing is the necessary second step which will get us somewhere.

Abraham finally overcame his fears to become what God had promised he would become.

The stories of the greats of Scripture are not of men and women who were fearless. They are stories of men and women who gave their fears to God, believed His promises, relaxed in His love and presence, and moved ahead.

For Further Reading

Irwin Lutzer. *Managing Your Emotions.* Wheaton, IL: Victor, 1986.

Duane Dyer. *Your Erroneous Zones.* New York: Avon, 1976.

Depression

What is depression?
Are all depressions alike?
What are the different types
of depressions?
How can depressions be relieved?

Lord, I've got a problem.
It seems that my whole outlook on life
has changed. I feel so sad all the time.
Is it possible that I am depressed? 🍏

"I've had it."
"I've failed."
"I want to die."
That's the language of depression.

Spiritual giants don't talk that way—or do they?

Would you believe that three of history's godliest men said those words and meant them? Three of the Bible's holiest heroes experienced depression.

The man who single-handedly brought Egypt to her knees, who wrote one-fourth of the Old Testament, who knew God face to face, and who gave us the Ten Commandments said: "I want to die."

His name was Moses.

The man who controlled Israel's weather by his prayers for seven years, who raised the dead, who fed the living, who unmasked a false god, who rebuked his king, who called down fire from heaven, and then slew all of his nation's false prophets said: "I want to die."

His name was Elijah.

The man who survived 72 hours in a whale's belly at the bottom of the Mediterranean, and then later preached to the world's most wicked nation, and saw 120,000 of earth's most evil heathens turn to God said: "I want to die."

His name was Jonah.

They were all depressed.
If you're depressed, you're in good company.

It took me seven years to publicly admit my depression.

In all those years I had never publicly described the
    sad
      empty
      lonely
        feelings of failure
that had invaded my spirit.

I had told only a few people of my voluntary commitment to the psychiatric ward of a veteran's hospital.

I had locked inside me the feelings of gloom and hopelessness that had caused me, at times, to despair for my life and, at other times, to even consider ending it.

I not only suffered the anguish of a disabling depression, but I believed some foolish notions about it.

Notions like "It is a sin to be depressed."

"Spiritual people never experience depression."

"Mental illness is always a sign of demon possession."

"Good Christians never need psychological counseling."

I have told my story of depression many times. Each time I share it, I am amazed at the large numbers of people who admit to me that they struggle with depression too.

Twenty million Americans suffer from depression annually.

Most of them struggle in silence.

I am equally amazed at the large numbers of people who know so little about this terribly complex illness.

What is depression?

Depression is an emotional illness characterized by mood swings that may vary from elation to deep gloom.

Depression is a feeling of being pressed down, gloomy, dejected, or sad. It often includes feelings of discouragement and inadequacy.

As with Moses, Elijah and Jonah, depression produces its own curious feelings of failure even when one is living in the glow of great success.

Like most depressed persons, during my periods of depression I was convinced that no one loved me, not even God.

Most of these symptoms have no basis in fact. But that makes no difference whatever to one who is depressed.

All depressions are not alike.

In fact, no two depressions are exactly alike. Causes and symptoms vary from patient to patient.

However, there are some general characteristics that apply to everyone. Here are several of them.

Anyone can get depressed, even a Christian.

The demanding stresses of life, the complex chemical construction of the human body, the genetic predispositions with which we are born, and the unpredictable reactions of the mind and body to the foods we eat can cause anyone at any time to become depressed.

Most Christians have difficulty admitting depression. Some deny it. Many hide it for fear that it would cause others to think less of them.

A Christian's spiritual resources can often help in limiting or relieving depression, but they do not guarantee immunity.

Depression is not terminal.

Depression can cause one to want to die, but it cannot kill.

Depression is always temporary.

A minor depression may last no longer than a headache.

A major depression may last for two or more years.

The wisest counsel I received during my stay in the hospital was given by a sympathetic and knowledgeable doctor who said, "It may take time, Mr. Baker, but you will get better."

Depression often requires help.

A severely depressed person is unable to help himself. All encouragement to "snap out of it" is in vain. It usually only complicates the problem.

Depression often responds to medication.

Many powerful and effective antidepressants are now available. They can often relieve a depression in a matter of days. I still take medication when I feel it is needed.

Depression is common.

Most people experience some form of depression in their lifetime. Even Jesus in His humanness displayed some of the symptoms of depression.

Depression can be dangerous.

A severely depressed person can lose touch

with reality, can destroy relationships and can commit suicide.

There are different types of depression.
Depressions can be classed as
  organic
    neurotic
    and reactive.

An *organic* or physical depression is often complex and usually requires the attention of professional medical help.
It is generated by certain biological changes from within and can be the result of
  chemical imbalances
    changes in the nervous system
    infections
    injuries
      drug or alcohol abuse.

Organic depressions can also be caused by
  childbirth
    menopause
    hypoglycemia
      or changes in body metabolism.
Glandular disorders such as low thyroid function can depress.
One of the chief causes of my depression was hypoglycemia or low blood sugar.
My first recommendation to anyone who requests help for depression is to consult a physician and request a complete physical examination.

A *neurotic* depression is usually caused by an emotional shock from which one does not allow himself to recover. He will brood until his depression becomes so severe that there is no relief without help.

A competent internist, counselor or biblically-oriented psychologist can usually provide the assistance that is needed.

Most depressions are *reactive*.

A reactive depression is triggered by a circumstance or event that causes one to experience or feel a sense of loss.

Depression may be introduced by the loss of
a job
a loved one
health
income
reputation
self-respect
energy
or independence.

Moses' depression was reactive.

An impossible workload, the constant griping of God's people over their dwindling water and food supplies, the forced marches in the unbearable heat of Sinai, along with the ever-present threat of enemy ambush finally got to Moses.

His feelings of
fatigue
discouragement
and depression

erupted in a torrent of words. Moses cried out:
"I alone am not able to carry all this
people, because it is too burdensome
for me. So if Thou art going to deal
thus with me, please kill me at once"
(Numbers 11:14,15).

God did not kill Moses.
Moses did not kill himself.
Instead God provided the tired leader with two
reasonable solutions to his problem.
First, God encouraged Moses to distribute his
workload among the elders of Israel.
And second, God relieved Moses of the
pressure of providing the nation's food supply.
In so many words, God counseled Moses to
take whatever corrective measures he could take
and then trust God for the rest.

When my workload is especially heavy, I find
the same solutions apply to me. There are ways in
which I can ease the pressure.
I can say "no" to added responsibilities.
I can enlist the help of others.
I can withdraw from impossible demands.
When no other human solution is available, I
can lean more heavily upon the resources that are
available to me from God.

Elijah's depression was reactive.
He was exhausted physically, spiritually and
emotionally.
He had just confronted the spiritual enemies of
Israel, engaged in a spiritual contest with 450 false

prophets, called down fire from heaven, and run 17 miles to escape the wrath of his wicked queen.

In addition to the strain of open conflict, Elijah felt deserted by his friends and believed that he had failed to restore Israel to her God.

Elijah was finished.

He walked deep into the wilderness, sat down under a juniper tree and requested that he might die. He said:

> "It is enough; now, O LORD, take my
> life, for I am not better than my
> fathers" (1 Kings 19:4).

Again, the divine counselor responded to the needs of a depressed man of God.

God put Elijah to sleep
  God fed him
    God encouraged him
      God reminded him that he was
        not alone
          God changed his job
            description.

No more confrontations with false prophets. Instead Elijah became the anointer of kings.

God gave him an assistant by the name of Elisha.

The pressure was off.

The depression lifted.

Elijah went back to work.

Jonah's depression was also reactive.

He was confused, bewildered and embarrassed.

Jonah had constructed his own system of beliefs and discovered that they didn't work anymore.

He believed that disobedience deserved death—yet he disobeyed and survived.

He believed whale attacks were fatal—yet he was swallowed alive and lived.

He believed wicked nations would be destroyed—yet the worst of all of them was spared.

He believed God could not love the Ninevites—yet He did.

Jonah had never before experienced the grace of God. The people he hated were being blessed. And furthermore, the little shade tree he needed in order to survive the intense heat withered and died.

He begged with all his soul to die.

"Death is better to me than life," he said.

Jonah was depressed.

His self-pity had consumed him.

A rebuke was necessary.

God reminded him that 120,000 eternal souls in the great and wicked city of Nineveh were of far greater value than the temporary little tree that had shaded him.

Reactive depression is caused by circumstances or events which provoke pressure and pain that we feel we don't deserve.

We blame God
we pity ourselves
and we withdraw into
a dark stupor.

A spiritual depression is reactive.

It's the response of the spirit to sin.

In Deuteronomy 28:65 the Lord promised depression in the event of disobedience.

He called it "despair of soul."

We call it "guilt."

Unrelieved guilt results in depression.

David the king was overwhelmed by the guilt of his sins of adultery and murder. His body wasted away, he sighed constantly and lost his energy and vitality.

His depression was a reaction to his sin. His depression lifted in response to his confession and forgiveness.

Judas' guilt was so heavy and his depression so great that he killed himself.

What can be done about depression?

Determine the cause.

I suspect the presence of depression when I am
　tired without a cause
　　sad without a reason
　　　hungry when I've just eaten
　　　　wanting to sleep when I just
　　　　got out of bed
　　　　　wanting to escape when I'm
　　　　　not being pursued.

I then search for the cause.
I often find the problem in
　a pile of unpaid bills
　　a list of unreturned phone calls

> a succession of sleepless nights
> a missed meal
> an unresolved conflict
> an unexpected criticism
> an unconfessed sin
> or even unwanted weight.

Depression clouds the thinking. Help is often needed in determining the cause. I secured over one hundred hours of professional counseling which was of great value to me in identifying the cause of my depression.

Acknowledge the depression.

Speak the word "depression."
Say it!
"I'm depressed" is awfully hard to admit. But acknowledging depression is necessary to finding its solution.

Resist the urge to withdraw.

When depressed, we are strongly tempted to
> hide under the covers
> run out the door
> stop the world and get off.

We can flee from the problem but not from the depression.

Correct the obvious.

Correct any problem you can identify.
I am constantly amazed at what happens to my mild depression when I correct an obvious problem I've been neglecting.

Completed projects, weight loss, a clean desk, or a healed relationship can often lift the spirit significantly.

Engage in physical exercise.

If no other form of exercise is possible, walk. Walking from one to three miles each day will improve the circulation, stimulate the metabolism and clear the mind.

Resist harmful drugs.

Depressants, relaxants, sleeping pills, and alcohol can deepen a depression.

A prescribed antidepressant, on the other hand, can often control and even lift depression.

Check your diet.

Caffeine and sugar are problems for me. They stimulate, excite and make relaxation and sleep difficult.

I eliminate them as much as possible, especially just before bedtime.

Watch your sleep habits.

A depressed person wants to sleep all the time. In reality, he can sleep none of the time.

It's difficult to fall asleep.

It's impossible to stay asleep.

When I can't fall asleep, it's usually because my mind is racing through some real or imagined problem.

I breathe deeply.
I count backward slowly from one hundred.
And I pray.
The breathing relaxes me.
The counting distracts me.
And in praying I let go of my problem and give it to God.

Try praising the Lord.

King David commanded his depressed soul to praise God even when it didn't want to. Praise is an act of the will and can be performed regardless of the feelings.

David said to his soul:

"Hope in God, for I shall again praise
Him for the help of His presence"
(Psalm 42:5).

Thank Him in your depression that the way you feel is temporary.

Remember that depression is a self-limiting ailment. It may take time, but you will get better.

For Further Reading

Don Baker and Emery Nester. *Depression.* Portland, OR: Multnomah Press, 1983.

Leonard Cammer, M.D. *Up From Depression.* New York: Pocket Books, Simon and Schuster, 1969.

Suffering and Pain

Why does God allow suffering?

*Is suffering and pain limited
to the sinful?*

*What comfort can someone give to
those who are suffering?*

Lord, I've got a problem.
Why is there so much pain
and suffering in the world?
I thought life would be easier
when I became a Christian.
It seems only to get harder. ❦

There was a man from Uz whose name was Job.

Job had it all.

He owned the biggest spread in the Middle East—

    seven thousand sheep
    three thousand camels

five hundred donkeys
     five hundred yoke of oxen
grazing contentedly as far as the eye could see.
     Job had
          a lovely wife
               a sprawling home with a view
               ten wonderful children
                    the honor of his community
                    the respect of his peers
                    the love of the poor
                         and the admiration of all.
     He was probably
          chairman of his church
          head of the local P.T.A.
          and president of the Rotarians.

As a reputable and honorable judge, Job
corrected those in error.
     As a man of unparalleled wisdom, Job
counseled the confused.
     As a person with great compassion, Job
comforted those who mourned.
     Job was "man of the year" in the land of Uz.

Job was a godly man. God said Job was one-of-
a-kind. He was a man who was
     genuine
          and honest
               and without blame.
     Job had it all. In his security he fully believed
that one day he would die quietly and peacefully
after a long and good life.

But suddenly and without warning, Job lost it
all.

In just one day
lightning killed all his sheep
thieves stole all his camels
all his donkeys
all his oxen
and killed his farm hands.
In just one day Job lost it all. The rich man had
become poor. However you want to say it
his stock market collapsed
his business failed
his creditors foreclosed
his lenders refused credit
he lost his job.
Job lost it all. The richest man in the East was
broke.

Then, again without warning, a tornado
struck. His son's home was destroyed with his
seven sons and three daughters entombed
inside.
Job was devastated.
In uncontrollable grief he ripped his robe from
his body, shaved the hair from his head, fell to the
ground, and sobbed.

The next day a new pain appeared. He awoke
from a restless sleep to find his body inflamed and
sore.
The spots were hot and tender to the touch.
They spread quickly over his entire body until he
was covered with one angry boil that stretched
from his head to his feet.
His bones ached
his legs began to bloat

his face swelled
   and his voice quavered.
His only relief came as he scraped his inflamed
flesh with a piece of broken pottery.
He was driven out of his home and his
community to the local garbage dump.
There he sat in the ashes and dung
   alongside the beggars and outcasts
      among the lepers and the dogs.

He was deserted by his friends and mocked by
his enemies.
His condition was so desperate, his appearance
so contemptible, his pain so continual that his wife
finally suggested that he kill himself.

Job would have presented a great problem to
the theologians of our day who tell us that God
wills for the righteous to be wealthy and healthy.
Job was miserable. Job was broke.
Like most of us, Job wondered "why?"
Sixteen times in the book that bears his name
Job asked that question.
   He asked it of himself
      he asked it of his wife
         he asked it of his counselors.
He repeatedly flung that little word into the
heavens in hopes that God would answer.

I've lost count of the times that same question
has been asked of me.
Parents who just lost their only son in a car-
pedestrian accident asked it.
Why?

A new bride whose husband lost both legs in a plane crash asked it.

Why?

A teenager whose parents were killed in an automobile wreck asked it.

Why?

A young father and mother whose first-born baby succumbed to crib death asked it.

Why?

The growing family of a successful executive permanently disabled by a stroke asked it.

Why?

And a 13-year-old hemophiliac terminally ill with AIDS asked it.

Why?

For many years I pretended to know the answers, or at least offered to look for them.

Not any more.

If I had been seated by the smoldering ashes of Uz's garbage dump alongside Job and his counselors, I probably would have been as perplexed as they were.

I would have wondered at the sudden collapse of Job's empire.

I might have questioned the genuineness of Job's relationship with God.

But I could not have spoken with the finality of Job's friends who said: "Job, God is punishing you because you have sinned."

Suffering and loss is not limited to sinful people.

The Bible doesn't teach it and human experience doesn't confirm it.

Some of the wealthiest and healthiest people I have known have been the most godless.

Some of the worst suffering I have seen has been endured by some of the greatest saints.

I really don't fear the question "why?" nearly as much as I fear those who pretend to know the answer.

Jesus refuted this suffering-comes-from-sin explanation when His disciples asked about a man born blind.

> "Who sinned, this man or his parents . . . ?"

Jesus bluntly answered.

> "It was neither that this man sinned, nor his parents; but it was in order that the works of God might be displayed in him" (John 9:2,3).

There is no one pat answer to the question of pain and suffering. There are many answers—and sometimes there are none.

It may be that I have sinned.

That's always a good place to begin. First Corinthians 11:30 teaches that sickness and even death may result from wrong living. A believer who fails to bring sin into judgment in his life, repent of it and forsake it may become ill and may die because of it.

It may be that God is allowing suffering to make me humble.

The apostle Paul claimed that the reason he had been given a "thorn in the flesh" (2 Corinthians 12:7) was to keep him from becoming proud.

I have been plagued with a blood sugar problem for most of my years in the pastorate. It's not only humbling, it's downright humiliating to constantly acknowledge this physical weakness.

It may be that suffering is allowed to make me dependent upon God.

Paul also learned that his weakness was allowed in order that he might discover the limitless strength of God's grace.

Being dependent can also be a blow to the ego. But often it's been in times of greatest weakness that I experience extraordinary flashes of divine power.

It may be that I'm being permitted to suffer just to make me better.

Suffering has a refining influence in our lives. Like metal, we need fire in our lives to increase our value. Metals are melted to purify them. And the greater the value of the metal, the hotter the fire must be to melt it. Lead melts at a relatively low temperature. Silver and gold require more fire. Platinum needs the most.

Suffering is the fire God often allows to refine the believer.

For those of us who wish to be used by God, it seems that the heat is never removed—only the temperature is changed.

It may be to teach me how to hurt with others.

Suffering teaches compassion. We really can't feel the pain of others until we first have felt it ourselves.

I understood virtually nothing about depression until I became depressed. In the agonizing months of my depression I found out how it felt. Since then compassion and empathy have been added to my knowledge about depression. I have personally entered into the suffering and, as a result, I have been able to help those who suffer.

A young man came to me after a service recently. "Thank you for saving my marriage," he said.

I had never met him before. But he had read my book on the subject of depression and had been dramatically helped by it.

It may be accompanying my desire to be more godly.

The entire book of 1 Peter teaches that the more godly we become in this godless world, the more intense will be our suffering.

It may be to teach me something about God.

Suffering was used for that purpose in Job's life. Prior to his disasters, Job only knew God from the perspective of prosperity. Through his suffering, Job's understanding of God became more intimate and satisfying.

Suffering may be for no significant reason whatever.

Suffering may simply be the result of
  living in a sinful society
    or being exposed to an
      infectious bug
        or just growing old.
What would I have said to Job in answer to his
perplexing question?
There is no sure answer.
Pain doesn't search for answers. It looks for
relief.
If it can't find relief, it desires compassion,
sympathy and comfort.
I probably would have said and done the same
things to Job that I have said and done dozens of
times to people in recent years.
I would have listened until he was finished.
I would have sat in silence as I searched for an
answer that wouldn't come.
I would have poured him a fresh glass of cold
water.
I would have offered him a Kleenex to wipe
his sores.
I would have smoothed the ashes beneath his
body and tried to find something to pillow his
head.
I would have reached out and placed my hands
on his encrusted arm.
I would have looked into his searching eyes.
And I would have wept.

Finally, I would have said to him, "Job, I don't
know. I don't know.
I don't know why God is allowing this pain.
It seems unfair.

Suffering and Pain

It seems unkind.

It must be terribly painful and horribly humiliating.

I'm deeply sorry.

I wish I could answer your question, but I really don't know why God is allowing this pain.

But I do know who.

I know who has allowed this and I do know there must be some reason. But I can't unlock the mind of God and show it to you.

I do know He loves you
  and He cares for you
    and He hurts with you
      but I don't know why.

Can you leave your question with God?

Can you just believe that deep within His sovereign wisdom and deep, deep within His loving heart is a purpose that He has designed especially for you?

And can you believe that this is one of those pieces that fits into the puzzle of God's perfect will to make the final portrait absolutely perfect and beautiful?

And can you pause just long enough to worship Him with the simple words
      'Thank you, Father
      Thank you, Father.'

Thank Him for what? For the pain?

No, not for the pain. But for the promise.

God's promise is that when it is all over, the pain will have accomplished something very wonderful in you. Remember

'All discipline for the moment seems not to be joyful, but sorrowful; yet to those who have been trained by it, afterwards it yields the peaceful fruit of righteousness' " (Hebrews 12:11).

For Further Reading

Paul Tournier. *The Healing Spirit.* Westchester, IL: Good News Publishers, 1979.

Philip Yancey. *Where Is God When It Hurts?* Grand Rapids, MI: Zondervan Publishing House, 1980.

Guilt

What are the causes of guilt?
What does guilt feel like?
How can guilt be relieved?

Lord, I've got a problem.
I'm hurt, but I'm not injured.
I'm sick, but my doctor can find no illness.
I'm afraid, but I'm not sure why.
Could my problem be guilt? 🍎

    David got caught in the adultery trap.
    This David was not just any old David. This
David was
     David the shepherd boy
      David the giant-killer
       David the general
        David the king.
    He was
     a singer

a poet
   an author
    a husband
    a daddy
      and a very religious man.

He was really special to God.
In fact, he was one of Jesus' great-great-
granddaddies.
Men like that don't do things like adultery.
Men like that are
   proper
    cautious
     discreet
      and terribly godly.

It was in the spring, when kings were
supposed to be busy.
But not David—not this year.
This year was different. David was
   too tired
    or too distracted
     or too old to fight.
He sent his soldiers into battle, but he stayed
home.

It was on one of those lazy, crazy days that
David spotted a woman
   next door
    in the bathtub.
She made him forget
   he was a king
    and a general
     and a husband

and a father
and a very religious man.
He went to bed with her.
Now adultery is pretty "heavy."
Adultery is not going to bed with *your* wife.
Adultery is going to bed with *someone else's*
wife.
God doesn't like that!
Neither does the husband—if he finds out.

What do you do if you go to bed with another
man's wife?
You quit! And if you're smart, you quit quickly.
If you can't quit
you lie to everybody
you worry
you hope
you cry
you look over your shoulder
and you hope nobody finds out.

If you're a king, or an absolute fool, you just
might go even further.
You might murder the competition.
Then you can move in with your bathing
beauty
and have kids
and pretend everything is
beautiful.

You may hide what's going on outside. But
how do you hide what's going on inside?
You put up a great front and wear a convincing
mask.

Guilt
73

You go through all the motions.
  You work
   you sleep
   you pray
    you pay the bills
     you go to church
      you even take your kids
       to the circus.
That's all on the outside.
Inside—you hurt.

David tells what it feels like—later, in Psalm 32.
  He lost weight
   he groaned
    he hurt
     he felt heavy
      he was tired—always tired
       no matter how much he slept—
        he was tired.
He learned to blame his symptoms on
 a headache
   or the pressures of being king
    or mid-life crisis
      and the people could handle that.

But then things started going wrong on the
outside.
A snoopy friend found out.
Snoopy friends always find out.
(Actually, God told on the king.)
And it didn't stop there—God made sure
everybody found out.

David's people didn't trust him anymore.

And then his kid died.
Two other kids got "in trouble."
And then David's great-big, grown-up son
decided that his daddy should be
 replaced
  or liquidated
   or something.
He started a war—against his own dad—and
pushed him off the throne and took over.
And then that great-big, grown-up son got
killed—speared while hanging from a limb by his
hair.

That son was special and his death hurt the
king.
David had finally had enough.
Who would have thought that one night in bed
with a neighbor-lady could have caused all this
trouble?

David decided it was time to do something—
something different, something other than
 cover up
  or pretend
   or take aspirin.
He sent the servants home early
 turned off the bell
  closed the drapes
   turned down the lights
    got down on his aching knees
     and talked to God.

David was quite a pray-er.
He could lift prayers higher than Mount Zion.

He had a real flowery way about him. And
whenever anything special was going on where the
people needed a good pray-er, everybody wanted
the king.

This time was different.
  No long prayers
    no flowery phrases
      no flowing sentences
        just four words—
          "Lord, I have sinned."
Kings are not used to saying things like that.
Kings like to say
    "The devil made me do it"
      "I just couldn't help myself"
        "I got loaded and didn't know what
          I was doing"
          "It was her idea"
            "I'm sorry, sir, I just can't
              remember."

He told God he had sinned.
He told his pastor he had sinned.
He told his wife he had sinned.
He told his family he had sinned.
He told his cabinet he had sinned.
He told his people he had sinned.

God forgave him.
And he stopped
  worrying
    crying
      lying
        and he even stopped
          looking over his shoulder.

He regained his weight.

His groaning stopped.

The pressure eased.

He even slept nights—and woke up rested.

But.

Even though David got his health back and his throne back, some things were lost—forever.

He never got his baby back.

His great-big, grown-up son—the one he loved—was dead.

His two kids never got over their shame.

His wife never forgot how the king murdered her first husband.

His people never forgot how their king had disappointed them.

The world will never forget David and Bathsheba. Their sin will live as long as people can remember.

David is remembered as Israel's greatest king—and history's most notorious adulterer.

His adultery is erased from the memory of God forever—that's forgiveness.

But his adultery lingers in the memory of man forever—that's life.

Guilt is heavy.

Guilt is the deepest source of human woe.

Guilt is the greatest cause of physical and psychological pain.

Guilt is the unavoidable pain one feels when he fails to do what he believes is right.

Guilt is heavy—but guilt is healthy.

It's a sign that our conscience is still alive.

It's a sign that God still loves us.

It's a sign that the Holy Spirit is still active within us.

How does one relieve guilt?

The guilt of sin is removed by confession.

> "If we confess our sins. He is faithful
> and righteous to forgive us our sins
> and to cleanse us from all
> unrighteousness" (1 John 1:9).

If guilt is doing to you what it did to David, do what David did.

He confessed his sin. He didn't try to excuse his sin, or to call it by another name. He confessed his sin.

"Lord, I have sinned."

Confession is followed by forgiveness.

To accept God's forgiveness is sometimes harder than to ask for it.

But God has promised not only to forgive, but also to forget.

> "And their sins and their lawless
> deeds I will remember no more"
> (Hebrews 10:17).

God has no memory of sin once it has been forgiven.

Forgiveness is followed by thankfulness.

God's forgiveness is so different from man's forgiveness that it's hard to believe and even harder to accept.

Sometimes our guilt is so heavy that we keep
asking for forgiveness when we have already
received it.
Rather than continually asking, begin
thanking
    repeatedly
     humbly
      and joyfully
       until its reality finally
        floods you with peace.

Confession is often followed by pain.

It's a different pain—an easier pain than guilt.
But it's still pain.
    It's the pain of
     embarrassment
      shame
       disappointment
        sorrow
        and distrust.
    It's pain—lighter than guilt and less permanent
than guilt. But it's still pain.
    It won't last forever, but that's very little
comfort when the pain hits.

Confession is followed by rebuilding

    trust
     relationships
      credibility
       family
        and life.

David was restored to God, but never completely to his family, his friends or his people. Some things are lost forever when sacred trusts are broken.

When one of my staff members fell into the adultery trap, we accepted the fact of God's forgiveness.

We also accepted the fact of man's distrust.

In order to help him rebuild his life and achieve complete restoration, we required that he
 tell his wife and family
  what he had done
   surrender his credentials
    not engage in any form of public
    ministry until the church leaders
    gave him permission
     remain in his present church until
     restoration was complete
     rebuild his family before he
      considered rebuilding his career.

He did these things—all of them—and today is back in the ministry, a wiser, more sober servant. But he is also a much more effective servant.

With confession, forgiveness and restoration, there is always one added word:
"Go, and sin no more" (John 8:11).

For Further Reading

A. Dudley Dennison, M.D. *Give It to Me Straight, Doctor.* Grand Rapids, MI: Zondervan Publishing House, 1972.

Vernon Grounds. *Emotional Problems and the Gospel.* Grand Rapids, MI: Zondervan Publishing House, 1976.

Temptation
❦

What does temptation feel like?
Where does it come from?
What is the purpose of temptation?
What forms do temptations take?
What provisions has God made
for our deliverance?

Lord, I've got a problem.
I want something I can't have.
I crave something that's not right.
I'm tempted to do something
I shouldn't do. 🍎

Joseph also got caught in the adultery trap—almost.

It happened on a sunny day in Memphis—Memphis, Egypt, that is.

The king was inspecting his troops in Kadesh.

Potiphar, head of his majesty's secret service, was at the king's side.

Potiphar was always at his side—
  day after day
   week after week

month after month—and often
night after night.

The king's bodyguard was an indispensable
commodity—a vital necessity to the king's
protection.
Potiphar's chief duty, and his only duty, was to
guard his king.
He performed his duty well—so well, in fact,
that
the promotions came
the duties increased
the time demands became
impossible.

Potiphar's wife was the perfect complement to
a husband on the rise.
She was
beautiful
exciting
gracious
witty
a sparkling addition
to any guest list.
Her home was spacious
her furnishings ornate
her servants efficient
her children well-behaved
and her duties minimal.

But she was bored
and she was lonely
and she was neglected
and she was resentful.
Then she met Joseph.

Joseph was handsome
  and sensitive
   and efficient
    and attentive
     and far from home
      and 30
       and he was there.

While Potiphar spent his days with the king,
his wife spent her days with Joseph.

Each morning, Joseph assumed his duties
managing the affairs of Potiphar. And each day
Joseph listened attentively to the frustrations of
Potiphar's wife.

Then it happened.

This young, exciting, lonely, neglected
housewife saw the solution to her problem of
loneliness in the young, handsome, sensitive,
attentive manager of her husband's affairs.

You realize as you read this, don't you, that
though this story is nearly four thousand years old,
it has all the ingredients of a typical contemporary
affair?

And you realize, don't you, that although
Potiphar's wife may have dreamed of a passionate
afternoon with her husband's employee, like most
dreamers, she hadn't really planned on it?

And although Joseph realized that his boss's
wife was demanding more of his time, and that she
was discussing subjects that were getting more
intimate, he really hadn't planned to have an affair
either.

Temptation

But like most affairs, this affair just happened—almost.

But let me finish the story.

One day when Potiphar was gone and Potiphar's wife was feeling especially lonely, Joseph entered to perform his usual duties.

Joseph and Potiphar's wife talked
and they talked
and they talked
until, without warning, she reached for his fingertips, looked into his eyes and said with characteristic modern-day boldness, "Come to bed with me."

Now Joseph may have been
young
and handsome
and sensitive
and attentive—
but he was no fool!

He was a man, with all the emotions and drives and desires of a man. But he was no fool.

He was the great-grandson of Abraham
the grandson of Isaac
the son of Jacob.

He was one of the original 12 who produced the 12 tribes of the nation of Israel, the little nation that would someday rule the world.

Joseph was not in Egypt by choice.

He was not in Potiphar's service by chance.

He had not become the trusted, devoted, honored servant by personal ambition.

He was where he was because of God.

Joseph wanted God's blessing and Potiphar's respect even more than he wanted Potiphar's wife.

How did Joseph respond to her invitation?
He reasoned with her.
He said, "Your husband has trusted me and my God has honored me—I cannot sin against either."
Sometimes reason works, but only sometimes.

She asked him again—every day.
When Potiphar was gone
   and the children were in school
      and the servants were distracted
         she'd say, "Come to bed with me."
Every day Joseph reasoned with her and every day he resisted her.
He'd say "no" as politely as possible.
Joseph would have resigned if he could have. But Joseph was a purchased slave. A job change was not an option.

The day came again when Potiphar was gone
   and the children were in school
      and the servants were distracted
         and the couple was alone.
Again they talked and talked.
Then, suddenly, the lonely wife of an ambitious husband reached for the buttons of Joseph's shirt.
This was not time for
   reason
      or resistance
         or resignation.

It was time to run.
Joseph ran.

To some, running away may seem to be the act
of a coward.
But to Joseph
the dreamer
with the coat of many colors
who spared Egypt
who saved Israel
and became one of Jesus'
ancestors
running was a mark of great spiritual strength.
And in today's sensuous culture, running is
probably the best way to resist temptation.

Temptation is the method Satan uses to arouse,
to entice and to persuade us to do something that
God has told us not to do.
It's the method the enemy uses when he wants
to destroy
a life
a family
a church
a job
or a reputation.
It's the method he used to destroy Adam and
Eve in their idyllic home in the Garden of Eden.
He has used it ever since to destroy nations.

Temptation is a simple method that takes what
is wrong and makes it look right.
It takes what is bad and makes it look good.

It takes what is dangerous and makes it look harmless.

It began in the Garden of Eden with two innocents who became the villains responsible for every calamity that has befallen humanity.

God had given everything in this world to Adam and Eve. He had withheld nothing—except the fruit of a single tree planted in the middle of the garden.

Satan focused their minds on God's single restriction and suggested that God was selfish to not give them everything.

He made the forbidden fruit look good, attractive and necessary. And he tried to make God look foolish.

Eve, and then Adam, yielded. They sinned and pulled the whole human race down with them.

Temptation's purpose is to cause us to do what God has told us not to do.

Temptation's strategy is to make wrong look right and bad look good.

Temptation's ultimate goal is to destroy.

There was another young man who faced temptation.

He also was
> young
> > and sensitive
> > > and efficient
> > > > and attentive
> > > > > and far from home
> > > > > and 30.

He had come to rebuild what Satan had destroyed.

He met the tempter, resisted the temptations and taught us everything we need to know to overcome temptation's power.

He taught us that temptation always strikes in one of three areas:
  the physical
    the psychological
      or the spiritual.

The physical temptation came first.

When Jesus craved food after a 40-day fast, Satan urged Him to abuse His power by using spiritual energy to satisfy a physical need.

"Turn stones into bread," the tempter said.

The flesh gets awfully hungry at times—and not just for bread. If we let it, the flesh will do anything to get what it wants.

Potiphar's wife was ready to sacrifice all that was sacred to satisfy her appetite for physical love.

The psychological temptation came next.

"Throw yourself down from the temple's pinnacle."

Jesus was tempted to do something impressive. What an impression it would have made to fall so far and to land unhurt.

We all want to be "somebody."

Our ego-needs urge us to seek recognition in some of the craziest ways. We want to look good— even great. We want to be praised and lauded. And many of us are unwilling to wait for recognition.

That's what the second temptation was all about—"make yourself look good, don't wait for God to do it."

The spiritual temptation came next.

"Who will be God in your life?" That was the question posed next.

"Worship me and you can have it all," he said as he pointed to the riches of earth.

That doesn't seem like much, does it: the whole world for the price of one single compromise?

That's what Satan suggested.

That's what Jesus resisted.

How did Jesus overcome His temptation?

Like Joseph, Jesus reasoned—but not with His own logic. He met each temptation head-on with the Scriptures.

Jesus resisted Satan's urgings to eat by reaching into His memory and pulling out Deuteronomy 8:3:

> "Man shall not live on bread alone,
> but on every word that proceeds out
> of the mouth of God."

To do what God says is more important than to have what I want. That was Jesus' answer, and it immediately exposed the deceit of the enemy.

When Satan misquoted Scripture to urge Jesus to throw Himself off the temple's pinnacle, He again reached into the Scriptures and quoted Deuteronomy 6:16:

"On the other hand, it is written, 'You
shall not tempt the LORD your
God.' "
Satan knows the Scriptures. He can even use
them to tempt us to do evil.

When Satan tempted Jesus to worship him,
Jesus responded with Deuteronomy 6:13:
"Begone, Satan! For it is written, 'You
shall worship the LORD your God,
and serve Him only.' "
Satan departed.

Only the Bible can unmask the enemy.
We can easily convince ourselves that physical
needs must be satisfied.
We can easily convince ourselves that ego-
needs must be satisfied.
We can easily convince ourselves that wealth
and power needs must be gratified.
Only the Scriptures can keep those needs in
check and reveal that even right things can be
secured in the wrong ways.
Only the Word of God can expose the
deceptions of Satan.

There are some things to remember about
temptation.

First, temptation is not a sin (James 1:14).

That's encouraging isn't it? Everywhere we
look in this present world we see something that
suggests sin to us. But the suggestion to sin is not
the same as the sin.

Second, temptation does not come from God (James 1:13).

God allows evil, but He never causes it.

Third, the power to resist temptation comes from God (1 Corinthians 10:13).

> "No temptation has overtaken you but
> such as is common to man; and God is
> faithful, who will not allow you to be
> tempted beyond what you are able,
> but with the temptation will provide
> the way of escape also, that you may
> be able to endure it."

Notice the obvious in this verse. Everybody has the same problem—temptation. But no temptation is greater than the power God has made available to us.

Fourth, the weapons have been provided.

Jesus used Scripture. So should we.
Jesus taught us to pray:
> "And lead us not into temptation"
> (Luke 11:4).

Pray the words which are part of the model prayer best known to mankind.
James encouraged accountability:
> "Confess your sins to one another"
> (James 5:16).

Share your temptation problem with a trusted friend. Ask him or her to
> pray for you
>   check up on you
>   and be available to you.

Today's temptations are too great to be
endured alone.

Christ provides compassion (Hebrews 4:15).
Believe it or not, Jesus had the same kinds of
problems. That's why the Bible says He was tempted
"in all things as we are, yet without
sin."
He understands
the pressure
the persistence
and the pain of being tempted.
He understands the subtle strategy with which
Satan attacks us.
He even knows how it feels to crave something
we shouldn't have.
And because He knows, He cares.
And because He cares, He helps.
He helps even when He knows how much we
want something we shouldn't have.
He helps even when He knows we sometimes
don't want His help.

And if His divine assistance is not apparent
during temptation, and if all else fails, do what
Joseph did.
Run!

For Further Reading

James Dobson. *Emotions: Can You Trust Them?*
New York: Walker and Company, 1980.
J. Dwight Pentecost. *Man's Problems, God's
Answers.* New York: Thomas Nelson, 1983.

Anger

Where does anger come from?
Is is ever okay to be angry?
Does God ever get angry?
How do I control my anger?
What is God's provision for anger?

Lord, I've got a problem.
When I get angry, I lose control.
No matter how hard I try, I blow it.
Can I ever bring my anger under
control? 🍎

Martha was mad.
Her only brother had died.
It was
  an unwanted death
   an unexpected death
    an unnecessary death.

Her brother was
  young
   robust

        in good health
           and godly.
     And people who are
        young
           robust
           in good health
           and godly
aren't supposed to die—we think.
     But Lazarus died.

     Martha did everything she could do.
     She loaded up on first century
        aspirin
           decongestant
           cold medicines
           vitamin C
           and chest rubs.
     She put Lazarus to bed
        kept him warm
           fed him chicken soup
           and placed hot-water bottles
           at his feet.

     She sat with him
        at night
           in the morning
           and around the clock.
     She prayed.
     She asked
        Mary to pray
           her church to pray
           and her friends to pray.

     She called the doctor—he came.
     She called her friends—they came.

She called her pastor—he came.
She called the family—they all came.
She called Jesus—but He didn't come.

Four days after Lazarus' funeral, Jesus finally arrived.

He was too late.

When Martha met Him on the road outside her hometown of Bethany, her anger spilled over and she greeted Him by saying,

> "Lord, if You had been here, my brother would not have died" (John 11:21).

Mary was mad too.

Mary was Martha's sister.

Mary was Lazarus' sister too.

Mary was the one who poured her costly perfume all over Jesus' feet.

She didn't even go out to greet Him.

She sat with the mourners.

When Jesus arrived, she fell at His feet weeping, and hurled the same accusation as her sister:

> "Lord, if You had been here, my brother would not have died" (John 11:32).

You'd think that close friends would come when a brother is dying.

You'd think that someone to whom you'd given your greatest treasure would respond when needed.

Jesus didn't come—until it was too late.

Both sisters were angry.

They both blamed Jesus for Lazarus' death.

Anger is like that.
It comes from the frustrated or frantic wish
that people or things were different than they are.
Mary and Martha wanted their dead brother
back.
They also wanted Jesus to show more
compassion than He had.
They wanted to change something they were
helpless to change, and to change Someone they
thought really didn't care.

Anger says,
  "I don't like the way I am"
  "I don't like the way you are"
  "I don't like the way life is."

Anger can be caused by anything from a
needle that can't be threaded to a world that won't
stop revolving.
We get angry at
  children who don't mind
    drivers who don't signal
      hammers that smash fingers
        keys that stay lost
          friends who are late
parents who are too protective
  pastors who are insensitive
    even God, if He doesn't
      give us what we want.
We also get angry with ourselves when we
don't or can't live up to our expectations.

Anger takes many forms from
  abusive language
    to ridicule
      to tantrums
        to physical violence.
Sometimes it's sarcastic.
Sometimes it's silent.
Sometimes it just slams the door and walks
away.

Anger has uses. It can frighten, manipulate,
and destroy.
It can delay rational decisions.
It can avoid facing problems.
It cannot build positive, healthy relationships.

It's true that
  God displays anger (Psalm 7:11)
    Jesus displayed anger (Mark 3:5)
      the Holy Spirit angered King Saul
        (1 Samuel 11:6).
But in every instance, God's anger is under
control.
It's out-of-control anger that is dangerous and
damaging.

Anger begins with a wish.
"I wish this light bulb would screw into the
socket like it should."
"I wish my husband would pick up his socks
like I do."
"I wish that car would get out of my way."
"I wish my baby would stop crying."

A wish, if not granted or controlled, turns to regret.

A regret turns to frustration.

A frustration turns to anger.

Anger then slips down into the soul and becomes bitterness, or spills out into the open in the form of hostility.

In his letter to the Ephesians, it sounds like the apostle Paul is encouraging anger when he says:

"Be angry, and yet do not sin; do not
let the sun go down on your anger"
(Ephesians 4:26).

He is not encouraging anger.

He is recognizing it as one of our human emotions and urging us not to let it get out of control.

When anger explodes and leaves human debris lying around, Paul is telling us to be sure to pick up the pieces and put them back together before going to bed.

To be angry and not sin is to:
recognize anger before it becomes
frustration
correct it before it becomes bitterness
control it before it becomes hostility
confess it before it turns into guilt and
creates distance.

Some anger needs medical attention. A tumor on the brain can cause uncontrolled anger.

Blood sugar problems can cause uncontrolled anger.

Most anger can be controlled, however.
Let me suggest some steps to follow.

Identify the cause of anger.

Ask yourself, "Why am I feeling angry?"
Getting in touch with the source of anger is of
primary importance. It can often defuse the feeling
before any damage is done.

Postpone your anger.

Wait! Instead of counting to 10, try 15 or 30 or
60. A little cooling-off time may save hours of
sadness.

Acknowledge your anger.

Say, "I'm feeling angry and I don't want to."
Admitting your feelings will sometimes provide a
springboard to discussion rather than dissension.

Keep a record of your anger.

There are "down" times in everyone's day. It's
good to recognize when these times occur and be
prepared to avoid their consequences.

Distract yourself.

When feelings of impatience begin to surface,
find an acceptable way to distract yourself from
them. Turn on the radio or TV, or read or even
balance the checkbook.
I was impatiently waiting for a red light to turn
green when I looked at the car next to mine. Its
driver, a dear friend, was holding a pack of

Scripture memory cards in his hand and reciting verses to himself.

Has it ever occurred to you that anger-provoking delays may be divine opportunities for prayer?

Deal with the anger.

Don't repress it or suppress it. Deal with it! Acknowledge its presence, delay it or distract it, or better yet, give it to God. Expressing anger in a healthy way is better than allowing it to turn into bitterness.

Alert others to your problem.

If you're struggling with anger, announce your problem to others. Tell them you're trying to gain control, but ask them to be patient with you in the event you fail.

Apologize after an outburst.

And do it quickly! Apologies may get old in a hurry to others who don't understand the monstrous problem of anger. But apologizing is necessary in order to condition yourself against further outbursts and to heal fractures that may occur.

Accept God's provision for anger.

The word "meekness" is God's divine provision for the problem of anger.

Meekness is the quality displayed by Jesus (Matthew 11:29).

Meekness is a condition for unity among Christians (Ephesians 4:2).

Meekness was a characteristic of Paul's ministry (1 Corinthians 4:21).

Meekness, sometimes synonymous with gentleness, means to accept all God's dealings without resistance or bitterness.

Meekness is the opposite of anger.

Anger wants to change things or people, remember?

Meekness accepts things and people as they are.

Meekness can be accepting because it acknowledges that God is the gracious controller of all things.

Meekness sees God at work in every circumstance of life.

Meekness sees God working in and through every person in our lives.

Meekness accepts the sovereignty of God.

Meekness believes that though God may not cause every event in life, He at least allows each of them.

If God has allowed something in my life, it must be for a positive purpose.

And if it is going to achieve something positive in my life, then I can accept it.

There is something very hideous and ugly in the manner in which Jesus died.

He could have resisted.

He could have retaliated.

He could have displayed intense hostility and anger against His murderers. If He had, we all would have felt He was justified.

Instead, He displayed meekness.

Peter described His response:

> "While being reviled, He did not
> revile in return; while suffering, He
> uttered no threats, but kept entrusting
> Himself to Him who judges
> righteously" (1 Peter 2:23).

That's meekness.

Jesus' response made forgiveness of sin and eternal life possible for us.

If you're struggling to develop a spirit of meekness like that, why not quit struggling and just accept it.

Meekness, or gentleness, is one of the personality traits of the Holy Spirit sometimes called the "fruit of the Spirit."

When we submit to the control of God's Spirit, meekness becomes one of our characteristics.

Let's go back to Martha and Mary for a minute.

They didn't like things as they were.

They wanted the events of the past few days changed.

They wanted their brother back.

They were angry because they could do nothing about it.

They were also angry because the One who could have helped them appeared disinterested.

When they finally "vented" their anger, they did so to God.

You'll notice as you read the story in John 11 that Jesus received their accusation twice.

But He didn't rebuke them, resist them, or even answer their complaints.

God understands anger.

He recognizes man's futility to make meaningful changes.

He understands when we're frustrated and disappointed with life.

He can handle our outbursts.

He can handle them much better than even our closest friend.

He can even forgive them.

Next time you're feeling angry, do what Martha and Mary did.

Tell Jesus!

I can guarantee you one thing—you won't have to pick up any broken pieces afterward.

For Further Reading

Wayne W. Dyer. *Your Erroneous Zones*. New York: Avon Books, 1976.

Erwin Lutzer. *Managing Your Emotions*. Wheaton, IL: Victor Books, 1986.

Worry

What is worry?
Do godly people worry?
What are the causes of worry?
What are the results of worry?
How can a Christian combat worry?

Lord, I've got a problem.
I'm a worrier. I worry about anything.
I worry about everything.
How can I stop worrying? 🍎

Paul the apostle worried.

Paul was the spiritual giant of the first century church.

Paul was the man who took the Gospel to the known world in one generation.

Paul was the preacher who stood boldly before kings and Caesars.

Paul was the writer of half the books of the New Testament. He was the one who told us how to live by faith.

Paul was the miracle-worker who could bring
life to the dead
health to the sick
sight to the blind
and hearing to the deaf.
But he worried.

People like that don't worry—we think.
People like that are above worry—or beyond
worry.
People like that live lives of serene,
undisturbed, uninterrupted faith—we think.
But Paul worried—just like anybody else.
And he told us about it.

It happened during one of his evangelistic
campaigns.
He had just finished a trip through a foreign
country.
It was a trip different from any he'd ever
taken.
He was called to preach.
He wanted to preach
He was ready to preach
And people were ready to listen.
But God silenced him.
It seemed to Paul that there were no job
opportunities for apostles in Asia Minor.
Paul was worried about his future.

He had another worry.
Just a few weeks earlier he had written a letter
of sharp rebuke to a very carnal church in Corinth.

In no uncertain terms Paul told them
they were wrong
they needed to repent
and God couldn't bless them
until they did.
He received no reply to his letter.
He was worried about what the people of
Corinth thought of him.

He had another problem.
He couldn't find Titus, his friend and traveling
companion.
Had Titus
become ill?
been lost at sea?
been waylaid by robbers?
deserted him?
Paul was worried that his best friend was lost
somewhere and desperately in need of him.

There are three very common causes for worry:
Where will my next job come from?
What will people think of me?
And what has happened to Titus—or
whoever it may be for you?

Paul described the effects of worry when he
said:
"I had no rest for my spirit"
(2 Corinthians 2:13)
He described his worried state again with the
words:
"Our flesh had no rest, but we were
afflicted on every side: conflicts

Worry

115

without, fears within" (2 Corinthians
7:5).
Paul's worries had caused in him
 a restless soul
  a weary body
   and a frightened heart.

Worry does that to people, even godly people
like Paul.
Worry, which is a twin to anxiety, can be
described as a state of fear or apprehension over
what may happen.
It is a disease of the spirit that immobilizes its
victims.
It causes hesitation, inaction, even retreat in
the face of an imagined event which, in most cases,
never comes to pass.
Someone has said:
"I have lived a long life, and seen lots
of trouble, but most of it didn't
happen."

Worry is disabling.

John Watson said in the *Houston Times*:
"What does anxiety do? It does not
empty today of its sorrow, but it does
empty today of its strength. It does
not make you escape evil; it makes
you unfit to cope with it."
Dr. W. C. Alvarez of the Mayo Clinic has said:
"Eighty percent of the stomach
disorders that come to us are not
organic, but functional. . . . Most of
our ills are caused by worry and fear."

Worry is useless.

Jesus brought the foolishness of worry into sharp focus with the question:

> "And which of you by being anxious
> can add a single cubit to his life's
> span?" (Matthew 6:27).

Worry is common.

It's a human disease that is encouraged by the society in which we live.

We equate worry with caring.

We think that worry is proof of love.

And we all worry about the same things:
children
health
dying
jobs
security
accidents
decisions
weight
money
bills
weather
aging
war
happiness
and reputation.

Some of us even worry because we have nothing to worry about.

Review the list above and take note of how many things we worry about that we have no control over.

Also take note of the things that could be eliminated from the list with just a little planning.

Paul was worried.

He was worried about the same things that worry us.

He was worried about his future, his reputation, and his friend.

What did his worry accomplish?

Nothing—but perhaps an upset stomach.

What actually happened?

Paul walked over to a seaport city called Troas, laid down and went to sleep.

While sleeping, God spoke to him.

God sent him to Europe where three things happened:

He led the greatest revival of his career

he learned that all was well in Corinth

and he found Titus.

Like all of us, Paul's worries were for nothing.

I'm anxiety prone.

I don't boast about it.

I'm not proud of it.

I certainly don't try to excuse it.

I have made real progress through the years, however, and for that I am grateful.

In my second pastorate I developed an "anxiety pain."

It was located right where most ulcers occur.

It was about the size of a half-dollar.

After repeated diagnostic tests it was determined that my pain was not organic but functional.

I sought counseling.

My counselor's first question was, "What are you worried about?"

It took weeks of very complex thinking to come up with a very simple answer.

My church was growing so fast that I was worried that it would grow beyond my ability to lead it.

I was worried about my job.

My worry displayed itself in
sleepless nights
frightened days
withdrawal
fatigue
and an anxiety pain
in the pit of my stomach.

My biggest problem was in determining the cause.

As soon as I understood the cause of my anxiety, the cure came easily.

I knelt beside my desk and asked God to forgive me.

My worry had been caused by my unbelief.

You see, it finally occurred to me that God knew where I was.

He knew how long I had been there.

He knew what had happened since my coming.

He knew my qualifications.

He knew my limitations.

He also knew what was yet to happen.

And He knew what I could and couldn't handle.

Now if God knew all this, and He did, then He would have been awfully stupid to put me in a place without the necessary equipment to do the job.

And God isn't stupid.

That's what I was suggesting by my worry.

That's why I had to apologize to God.

He forgave me.

The church continued to grow.

My anxiety pain left and has never returned.

A few years ago my doctor discovered the presence of cancer in my body.

It was a melanoma—the deadliest kind.

I smiled and thanked him for his efficient diagnosis.

I said good-bye to his nurse.

I greeted a friend at the waiting room door.

I climbed into my car, started the engine and drove. I drove and drove—for nearly two hundred miles before I was able to regain my composure enough to tell my wife.

After many days of anxious withdrawal and fear, I went back to my doctor and pumped him with questions.

"What's the procedure for removal?"

"How long will the surgery take?"

"Where will it be performed?"
"Will you be there?"
"What are the odds in favor of recovery?"
"How long will I be laid up?"
"What will the scar look like?"
"When will I be certain of complete recovery?"
"How can I be sure of your ability?"
"Have you ever had cancer?"

The more I know, the less I worry.

The doctor answered each question patiently
and thoroughly.
He drew diagrams.
He gave me material to read.
He then showed me a lengthy scar on his right
hand—his surgical hand.
"It was a cancer," he said. "And I know how
you're feeling."
Information and sympathetic understanding
went a long way toward relieving my anxiety.
In fact, I think the cancer was removed more
easily than was the worry.

I've found two things that help relieve anxiety.
They are the suggestions I've just mentioned:
Determine the cause of your worry and learn all
you can about the object of your worry.
Let me give you another suggestion.
Since worry is a mental exercise, try fortifying
your mind with the promises of God.
If you're worried about daily needs,
Philippians 4:19 might help:

"And my God shall supply all your
needs according to His riches in glory
in Christ Jesus."

Or if you're worried about any of the
necessities of life, you might try Matthew 6:25,26:
"For this reason I say to you, do not
be anxious for your life, as to what
you shall eat, or what you shall drink;
nor for your body, as to what you
shall put on. Is not life more than
food, and the body than clothing?
Look at the birds of the air, that they
do not sow, neither do they reap, nor
gather into barns, and yet your
heavenly Father feeds them. Are you
not worth much more than they?"
If understanding, information and Scripture
input aren't enough, you might try the Apostle
Paul's solution.
The man who had been concerned about
his future
his reputation
and his friend
was in jail awaiting execution when he wrote this
little gem.
He said:
"Be anxious for nothing, but in
everything by prayer and supplication
with thanksgiving let your requests be
made known to God. And the peace of
God, which surpasses all
comprehension, shall guard your

hearts and your minds in Christ Jesus"
(Philippians 4:6,7).

He tells us to do three things:
  Be anxious for nothing
    be prayerful for everything
    be thankful for anything.
That prescription, taken faithfully, produces
peace.
  God will faithfully place a guard about your
mind and cause you to be at rest.

During World War II, an elderly English
woman was the envy of all who knew her. Every
night, along with her neighbors, she made her way
to a nearby bomb shelter.
  But unlike the others, she spread out a
blanket, lay down and went right to sleep.
  When asked how she could sleep through the
nightly bombings, she replied, "My Bible says that
God never slumbers nor sleeps. I can't see any
reason for both of us staying awake, can you?"

And if
  understanding
  information
    Scripture input
      and prayer aren't enough,
then Peter gives us one more suggestion:
        "Casting all your anxiety upon
        Him, because He cares for you"
        (1 Peter 5:7).
Why not just give it to God?

For Further Reading

Wayne W. Dyer. *Your Erroneous Zones.* New York: Avon Books, 1976.

Erwin Lutzer. *Managing Your Emotions.* Wheaton, IL: Victor Books, 1986.

David V. Sheehan, M.D. *The Anxiety Disease.* New York: Bantam Books, 1983.

Disappointment

*What should be done
when a Christian leader falls?*

*Are fallen leaders
ever qualified to lead again?*

How can we avoid disappointment?

How can we prevent our own failure?

Lord, I've got a problem.
I'm disappointed.
I'm not sure I can trust anyone anymore.
I'm not sure I can trust myself.
Why are so many Christians—
even our leaders—falling into sin?
What can we do to help them?
How can we help ourselves? 🍏

Israel wanted a king.
Every country had a king.
 Egypt had a king
  Babylon had a king
   Canaan had a king.
But Israel had no king.

They had a country
  they had a capitol
    but they had no king.
Moses was dead
  Joshua was dead
    the Judges were dead.
Israel had a prophet
  but they wanted a king.

God had been Israel's king, but God didn't
wear
    a robe
      and a crown
      and a sword.
And God didn't
  stroll through Israel's streets
    and greet the people
    and kiss the babies.
The people wanted a king—one they could see
and touch and hear and be proud of.

So they asked Samuel the prophet to get them
a king.
  The king they got was Saul.
Saul was the
  handsomest
    strongest
    tallest
      bravest
man in all the land of Israel.
  Samuel anointed him
    God changed him
      the Spirit filled him

and all the people cried
"Long live the king."

Saul the king
  rallied his armies
    led them into battle
      defeated the enemies
        and enlarged the kingdom.
Then he "blew it."
He just couldn't do what God told him to
do, and he kept doing what God told him not
to do.
  Finally, God had to replace him.
So the
  handsomest
    strongest
      tallest
        bravest
man in all the land of Israel
  embarrassed his God
    shamed his people
      humiliated his family
  lost his mind
    attempted to murder his successor
      and finally killed himself.

Things like that happen often to leaders.
Things like that happen
  to presidents and governors
    to mayors and candidates
      to generals and colonels
        to pastors and popes
          to T.V. evangelists
            and parents.

Disappointment
129

And things like that can even happen to us.
Maybe that's why God reminds us:
"It is better to take refuge in the
LORD than to trust in man. It is better
to take refuge in the LORD than to
trust in princes" (Psalm 118:8,9).

Do we have the right to expect more from
ourselves and our leaders?

Absolutely!
The Bible's standards are high.
Christians are expected to be different.
Qualifications for Christian leaders are outlined
in 1 Timothy 3 and Titus 1.
Leaders are to be
   above reproach
    morally pure
     temperate
      prudent (sensible)
       respectable
        hospitable
         not addicted to wine
    not a fighter
     gentle
      not quarrelsome
       not covetous
        head of controlled families
         mature in the faith
          of good reputation
    not resentful
    not self-willed
     not quick-tempered
      a lover of good

> just
> > devout
> > > self-controlled.

These are demanding requirements.
They teach that Christians are to be more than talented and loving.
Christians are to be holy and blameless.

What do we do when Christians fall into sin?

We restore them quickly and cautiously.
> "Brethren, even if a man is caught in
> any trespass, you who are spiritual,
> restore such a one in a spirit of
> gentleness; looking to yourselves, lest
> you too be tempted" (Galatians 6:1).
We restore even if a man (or a woman) is *caught* in a trespass.
We restore even when there is no question of guilt.
And notice: the word is *restore*, not *punish*.
We are to restore them cautiously, realizing that what has happened to them could happen to us.

How do we restore them?

Matthew 18:15-17 describes the process we are to follow in restoring a fallen Christian.
> "And if your brother sins, go and
> reprove him in private; if he listens to
> you, you have won your brother. But
> if he does not listen to you, take one
> or two more with you, so that by the
> mouth of two or three witnesses every

fact may be confirmed. And if he
refuses to listen to them, tell it to the
church; and if he refuses to listen even
to the church, let him be to you as a
Gentile and a tax-gatherer."

If your brother sins, go.

The passage commands confrontation, not
cover-up.

Go is not an option. It is mandatory. We are to
engage in a rescue operation as soon as our
brother's danger is perceived.

Reprove him in private.

The purpose of the confrontation is to make
him aware of his sin and to affect correction, not to
expose him.

We are to tell no one.

If he listens to you, you have won your brother.

The church's goal is always restoration, not
exclusion. We set out to win, not to lose, the
sinning individual.

If he does not listen, take one or two more with you.

Our duty is to gently apply pressure by
expanding the knowledge of the offense to "two or
three witnesses," and eventually "to the church."

Let him be to you as a Gentile and a tax-gatherer.

If he still persists in his sin, the sinning
member is to be excluded from fellowship as if he
were an unbeliever.

This discipline is for all—leaders and followers alike.

Such discipline is painful, but necessary.

It is the only way of restoring a fallen believer.

Are fallen Christians ever qualified to serve again?

Certainly!

Do you remember Simon Peter?

Peter denied Christ—three times. And it would appear from Jesus' words in Matthew 10:33 that denial might even have been considered a greater sin than adultery.

But according to John 21:15-17, Jesus restored Peter and returned him to his position of leadership.

The demands on people in positions of public trust are great.

Restoration takes time. The process of healing is often slow. The healing must be complete before responsibility can again be assumed.

Sometimes the confidence one betrays is so great or the genuineness of one's repentance is so suspect that full restoration to a significant leadership role is impossible.

How can we avoid being disappointed?

We really can't—completely.

Our attachments to people are great, especially to those who minister to us. It hurts us when they fall.

We can lessen the disappointment if we can
learn a few simple principles.

First, expect perfection only from God.

Idols fall hard and smash easily.
In the days of Samson, the enemies of Israel
had their own Old Testament Buddha.
His name was Dagon.
   He was big
     he was popular
       he was located in a temple
         he was worshiped
           he was made of stone.
When Samson pulled down the pillars of the
temple, the roof caved in and Dagon was smashed
to bits.
When Dagon died, thousands of his
worshipers died with him, and the religion of the
Philistines also died.

That's why God warned us against idols.
Idols fall and idols die.
Much of present-day Christianity is idolatrous.
It revolves around personalities, not around God.
To lift man higher than he should be lifted
does two things.
It causes him to fall and it causes us to be
disappointed.

Expect perfection only from God.
Save your worship only for God.
   "It is better to take refuge in the
   LORD than to trust in man" (Psalm
   118:8).

Second, support only those ministries that are proven worthy.

Reject any ministry that refuses to be financially accountable.

If they won't open their books to you, don't open your heart to them.

Contributing funds to the financially careless may be a contribution to a ministry. But it eventually is a contribution to that ministry's collapse.

Third, support, encourage, and promote your local church.

The Church is God's institution to do His work on earth. God organized it with the built-in safeguards necessary to keep it pure.

Fourth, examine the character of Christian leaders before you support them.

Do they meet the qualifications of 1 Timothy 3 and Titus 1?

Are their lives above reproach?

Are their methods biblical?

Is their doctrine pure?

If they meet these qualifications, the chances are better that they will not disappoint you. But remember to expect perfection only from God.

Fifth, pray for those in leadership.

If Satan can cause our public servants to fall, he has weakened us all.

Sixth, pray for one another.

If those who lead us can fall, none of us is above sin and failure.

But if even those who lead us and fall can be restored, then anyone who has failed can be forgiven and restored to some form of service to our Lord.

How can we avoid our own failure?

Again, a few simple guidelines will help us stay on the right path.

First, believe the truth about our humanity.

The apostle Paul was
  old
    imprisoned
     experienced
     and godly
when he warned us to
     "put no confidence in the flesh"
     (Philippians 3:3).
Never trust the flesh.
Never think you are above sin.
Flesh is always flesh.
Flesh never improves.
Flesh is never tamed.
We will be truly safe from the flesh only when it is dead.
The most dangerous time in a believer's life is when he feels he is out of danger.

Second, adopt a practical solution to private sin.

Restrict your own privacy.
Jesus always sent His disciples out in pairs.
Do your counseling in teams.
Do your visitation in teams.

Third, memorize Scripture.

Sin begins in the mind.
So does holiness.
Romans 12:2 tells us that spiritual
transformation is the result of filling the mind with
Scripture.

Fourth, learn to walk in the Spirit.

Galatians 5:16 promises that if we walk by the
Spirit we will not carry out the desire of the flesh.

Finally, if you fall, repent and recover quickly.

Falling is a part of learning to walk.
That's true of spiritual walking too.
If you fall, accept God's forgiveness, pick
yourself up quickly, and start walking again.

Have you been disappointed by
  your pastor?
    your favorite T.V. evangelist?
      your "Christian" legislators?
        yourself?
Forgive them.
Forgive yourself.
And focus your attention on the One who
never disappoints.

For Further Reading

Don Baker. *Beyond Forgiveness*. Portland, OR: Multnomah Press, 1984.

Carl Laney. *A Guide to Church Discipline*. Minneapolis, MN: Bethany House, 1985.

Bill Bright. *How to Be Filled with the Spirit*. San Bernardino, CA: Campus Crusade For Christ, 1981.

Divorce

How does God feel about divorce?
What should be the church's attitude
toward divorce?
Are divorced Christians
ever again qualified for ministry?

Lord, I've got a problem.
I'm divorced and I'm lonely.
I can't find a church that will love me
or a place to serve
that will fulfill me. 🍀

Moses was a murderer.
As the pharaoh-elect of Egypt, he had been party to the
slavery
persecution
and death of Hebrew captives.

As a would-be protector of the same Hebrews, he killed an Egyptian.

Moses murdered the Old Covenant children of God in much the same way that Paul murdered the New Covenant children of God.

Both became God's most successful servants.

Both assumed positions of unparalleled leadership.

Moses wrote one-fourth of the Old Testament. Paul wrote one-half of the New Testament.

What a tribute to the
  amazing grace
    forgiving love
     and sovereign wisdom
of Jehovah God.

I made the above observations during a Sunday morning sermon on the life of Moses.

An unsigned hand-written note was on my desk when I returned to my office. It read:

    "It's a good thing Moses was only a murderer. If he'd been divorced he would never had been asked to serve the Lord."

In just 23 words an unnamed Christian had stated what may well be the Church's number one present-day dilemma.

The Church today is populated with some people who have committed an act—divorce—that the Church has long been telling people to avoid.

Our dilemma: How do we make divorced people feel comfortable without encouraging divorce? And how do we use divorced people in ministry without compromising the Scriptures?

First of all, let's remember that

God hates divorce (Malachi 2:16)
   the married hate divorce
     the divorced hate divorce
       and their children hate divorce.
And yet, with all this hate, nearly half of all marriages end in divorce. And even with God's strong disapproval of it, nearly as many Christians as non-Christians experience divorce.

No one entered adulthood or marriage planning to get a divorce.

No one who has lived through a divorce encourages another to pursue one.

There is no pain in all the world like the pain of a divorce.

It's the pain of failure without the hope of success.

It's the pain of fear without the hope of deliverance.

It's the pain of disease without the hope of recovery.

It's the pain of rejection without the hope of acceptance.

It's the pain of loneliness without the hope of a companion.

It's the pain of desire without the hope of fulfillment.

It's the pain of darkness without the hope of morning.

It's the pain of death without the hope of heaven.

It's the pain Hagar felt as she sat on the sun-parched sands of Beersheba waiting for her son to die. She had

no husband
no home
and no hope.
It's the pain of the bewildered Samaritan woman who had tried for happiness six times— and had failed.

I have watched more times than I wish to remember as the strands of a marriage began to loosen, as the knot slowly became untied, and as each individual string stretched and snapped.
I have seen the ecstatic joy of two people becoming one, and then the unparalleled pain as they became two again.
I have heard
    the sobs of helplessness
      the screams of anger
        the cries for help
          the pleas for forgiveness
            and the wishes for death.
I have felt
    the confusion of a child
      the shock of a parent
        the rejection of a wife
          the guilt of a husband
            and the clumsiness of a church.

I have sensed the sorrow of a son who's lost his best friend and the anger of a daughter who's lost her greatest hero when Dad moved away.
I have witnessed the sorrow and anger as they have burrowed their way deep into the souls of hurting children to

Divorce

remain there
   and fester there
   and grow there
until they overpower the hurting ones with another
personal disaster.

There is no pain like the pain of a divorce. It is
  pervasive
   continuing
    and infectious.
It has touched more lives and destroyed more
humans than any disease in history.

Is it possible that God hates and warns against
desertion and divorce because of the pain it causes
His creatures as well as because of the moral
breakdown it brings to His world?

God hates divorce, but loves the divorced.

Have you studied Him in Genesis 21:9-21 as He
took time out from governing the universe to visit
with that little servant-girl in the wasteland of
Beersheba?

God picked up what Abraham had thrown
away, saved the life of her son and gave hope to
the rejected mother.

Have you studied John 4:7-30 to see how Jesus
took time out from saving the world to meet with
Samaria's most miserable woman?

He told her how to find the happiness she
sought. Then He gave her
  His life in spite of her failures
  His joy in spite of her sins
   and His ministry in spite of
   her reputation.

Though God loves the divorced, His Church struggles to do the same.

There's been great improvement in the Church's capacity to love the divorced. But it hasn't happened as much from increased compassion as from the Church being overwhelmed by the increased numbers of divorced people coming through her doors.

We have been forced to rethink, restudy and reconsider both our theology and our relationships. This exercise has been good for all of us.

In my first church, there were no divorced persons attending to my knowledge.

My theology of divorce was quite simple.

I never encouraged divorce.

I never remarried the divorced.

I never associated with the divorced.

Today our churches are filled with divorced people. We are forced to grapple with weightier questions like, "Should divorced and remarried church members be allowed to lead, to preach or to pastor?"

We ask, "Can the blood of Jesus completely cover the sin of divorce?"

We ask, "Can the grace of God fully cover the sin of divorce?"

We ask, "Can the ministry of God be entrusted to those who have failed in marriage?"

I answer "yes" to all three of those questions.

In each church I have pastored, the traditional stance has been that no divorced and remarried person would be nominated to the office of pastor, staff member, deacon, deaconess, or elder.

Every year I would meet with the nominating committee and every year the questions regarding divorced individuals would be raised.

Every year I would say the same thing.

"The standards for ministry must be kept high. The tradition of this church has excluded the divorced from its five top offices.

"We have done this on the basis of our interpretation of 1 Timothy 3:2,12 and Titus 1:6. The qualification states that a leadership candidate must be the husband of one wife.

"Our interpretation of that passage has been that a church leader should never have been divorced and remarried.

"I believe that the Scriptures are saying something far different and far more binding than our traditional interpretation.

"But we must decide whether or not we want to pursue an intensive study of the Scriptures in order to change our conviction. And we must decide if we want to impose that study on the church to challenge its tradition.

"A change in theology, especially on an issue as emotionally charged as this one, requires time and energy, and it poses risks.

"Is this the year we want to expend the time and energy, run the risks and entertain change?"

In some churches where I posed the question, the issue of divorce and leadership was studied and changed. In other churches we left the issue alone.

When the apostle Paul stated that a church leader must be the husband of one wife, he was not discussing the marital history of the candidate. Rather, he was referring to the individual's present character.

Being the husband of one wife means that a man is "a one-woman sort of man."

A member of one of my former churches had been married at age 17 and divorced within one year.

Later he became a Christian and he remarried.

For 35 years he was a model husband, a loving father and a faithful Christian.

He was a gifted teacher. As a professional in education he influenced scores of people to trust and serve Jesus Christ.

Upon his retirement I wanted him to join our church staff.

The problem: He had been divorced.

For 35 years he had proven himself to be
  changed
   faithful
    and deserving.

He was not flirtatious, sexually distracted or in need of satisfying a fragile ego. He was "a one-woman sort of man."

But he had been divorced.

After considerable discussion it was decided that his present character was more important than his past history.

He joined the staff.

One couple I know was married after each of them had suffered through separate divorces. But

after ten years they have proven that they qualify
for church service.

They are
  discreet
    chaste
      and faithful.

They display a gifted ability to minister to
divorced persons.

They spearhead a divorce-recovery ministry
which has changed hundreds of lives.

They both meet scriptural qualifications for
church leadership.

But because they have each been divorced,
they are not permitted on the church staff.

The Church has dismissed a large segment of
its population to the status of spectator even
though they have
    repented of their sin of divorce
      received God's forgiveness
        and proven that their present
          character qualifies them
            for service.

The emphasis of biblical qualifications is on
present character, not on past history.

If qualifications for service in Paul's day had
been applied to past history, perhaps none of the
Christians described in 1 Corinthians 6:9-11 would
have been approved.

Conversely, if qualifications for service today
were correctly applied to present character, perhaps
many of today's leaders would not qualify.

There is forgiveness for divorce.

There is restoration after divorce.

There is happiness after divorce.

There is ministry after divorce.

That's what the blood of Jesus is all about.

That's what the message of redemption and reconciliation teaches.

That's what the power of divine forgiveness accomplishes.

The rejection experienced from a divorce should not be prolonged or worsened by rejection from a church.

The Church is God's spiritual hospital designed not to compound our injuries but to heal them.

The Church's responsibility in seeking leaders is to discover men and women of character.

Dr. Stanley Ellisen, in his book *Divorce and Remarriage in the Church*, lists the required character traits as

> good moral character
> good domestic relationships
> respectable social relations
> proper spiritual priorities
> and a sober and mature view
> of life.

Some people who have fallen, repented and been forgiven and restored may better qualify in these five areas than others who have never felt the intense pain that sin can cause.

The Apostle Peter was not ready to fulfill his role as the dynamic and powerful leader he became until after he had felt the pain of failure and the sweet, sweet peace of forgiveness.

The divorced are not disqualified from serving solely on the basis of their divorce any more than the nondivorced are qualified to serve because they are married.

Biblical qualifications stress present character, not past history.

One of my former staff members was discovered to have adultery in his history.

When confronted he
  acknowledged his sin
   confessed his sin
    forsook his sin
     restored his family
      rebuilt his life
      and returned to his ministry
with God's blessing, my blessing and the church's blessing.

Sinlessness doesn't qualify anyone for service because there is no such thing as a sinless Christian.

Forgiveness, restoration, consistency, and a developing spiritual character which honors God are the Bible's qualifications.

For Further Reading

Stanley A. Ellisen. *Divorce and Remarriage in the Church.* Grand Rapids, MI: Zondervan Publishing Company, 1977.

Lewis R. Rambo. *The Divorcing Christian.* Nashville: Abingdon Press, 1983.

H.S. Vigeveno and Anne Claire. *No One Gets Divorced Alone.* Ventura, CA: Regal Books, 1987.

Amy Ross Young. *By Death or Divorce . . . It Hurts to Lose.* Denver: Accent Books, 1967.

Aging

What are the stages of aging?
Who old is old?
Are there advantages to aging?
What opportunities await the aging?
What are the disadvantages
to growing older?
How can one grow older gracefully?

Lord, I've got a problem.
As difficult as it is to admit,
and as impossible as it is to prevent,
I must confess:
I'm growing older! ❦

Eighty is old.
Not to an 80-year-old perhaps.
But 80 is old to
   a 20-year-old
      a 40-year-old
         and even a 60-year-old.
Eighty-year-olds seldom go hunting for a job.
New careers usually don't begin at 80.
New fortunes usually are not made after 80.

New families usually are not formed after 80—except in the case of a man like Moses.

By all human standards, when Moses turned 80 it was time for him to search out a full-service, retirement center, plunk down his money, and move in.

After 40 years of leading the armies of Egypt all over the Middle East, and then 40 years of leading his father-in-law's sheep all over Sinai, it was time to quit. It was time to hang up the sword and the staff and take it easy.

I've been thinking similar thoughts recently.

Oh, I'm not 80. But then I'm not 40 anymore either.

Recently I took my first trip to the local Social Security Administration office.

I entered through the glass doors, looked at the waiting room filled with people, pulled number 34 from the "please take a number" rack, and sat down.

The room was large, bright, and cheerful. The seats were close together, but not uncomfortable.

An American flag stood in the corner. Dusty venetian blinds shaded the tall windows.

A number of tables were scattered about the room. Application forms and pencils were spread on top of them.

Directly in front of me was a large poster asking if I wanted to file for food stamps.

Many of the people in the room were poor. Most of them looked old.

They were all very quiet.
I wasn't poor.
I didn't feel old.
I didn't want to be there.
I didn't need food stamps and I was beginning
to feel that I didn't want Social Security benefits
either.
I jotted down a list of questions I wanted
answered.
How much money would I receive at age 62?
How much at age 65?
How much would both my wife and I receive?
How much could I earn in wages without
affecting my Social Security income?
Does income from another retirement program
count against my earnings?

While I waited I scanned folders and
pamphlets that were available to me.
One of them told me how to figure my own
Social Security earnings. I read it carefully,
followed the steps, and finally gave up in total
confusion.

The clerk called for number 34.
Her smile was warm and disarming.
She asked me to state
  my name
   my age
    my birthday
     and an estimate of
      last year's earnings.

She then informed me that, since I was 60, the information I requested could be secured immediately.

I was surprised.

Every question was answered completely and efficiently.

I was eligible for more than I had expected.

The entire process was quick and simple.

The clerks were far more friendly than I had expected.

They even called me "sir."

The interview took less than 30 minutes, even without a prior appointment.

As quick and simple as the procedure had been, I must admit that there was some pain involved. As soon as I stepped through those glass doors I made a statement—a painful statement—to myself and to the watching world. "I am getting older," I said.

How old is old?

Aging, like death, is something that only happens to others.

Someone has said that there are really only three stages in human life—
   youth
    middle age
     and "you haven't changed a bit."
I'm in the "you haven't changed a bit" time of my life. I look at myself in college pictures, wedding pictures, and a host of family photos

which span many years. I see very little change.
Others look at them and ask, "Who's that?"

Aging is something that only happens to
others—I thought.

As the anniversary years pile up, the children
move into their 30s, the grandchildren enter
school, and more and more family members depart
for Heaven, I must admit that I am growing older.

But I don't feel old.

I feel like a young man.

I think like a young man.

Sometimes I even act like a child.

Old age must be a state of mind—a state that I
haven't entered yet.

When asked to define old age
  people under 30 say 63 is old
   people 30-39 say 67 is old
    people 50-57 say 71 is old
     people 60-64 say 73 is old
      people 65 say 75 is old.

It seems that I'm not the only one having
difficulty with growing older.

There are many advantages to aging.

Some discounts are available.

This is only an advantage if you are willing to
admit your age.

I struggled with this at first. My problem now
is that when I ask for a senior citizen's discount, no
one asks me for proof.

I have joined the American Association for Retired Persons (AARP). They publish an excellent magazine and have a good emergency road service program available to their members.

For many, growing older includes the joy of grandparenting.

I used to think this was a myth. Not any longer.

One of my grandsons grabbed my hand recently, looked up into my face, and said, "Grandpa, you're my best friend."

His mother commented later that the only other "best friend" he claimed was Jesus.

The longer you live, the longer you can expect to live.

A man of 65 can expect to live another 13 years.

A man of 75 can look forward to another nine years.

A woman of 65 can expect to live another 17 years.

And a woman of 75 can expect to live another 12 years.

Sociologists today refer to those between 65 and 75 as the "young old" and those over 75 as the "old old." Judging by some of the well-preserved "old olds" I've seen, I can hardly wait!

There are many opportunities for older persons.

Aging increases wisdom
aging provides experience
aging gives perspective
aging reveals the "big picture"
of life.
It nurtures compassion
it produces discernment
and good judgment
it mellows
it matures.
It usually makes one easier to live with and
easier to love.

Age is becoming less and less of a barrier in
government and industry. It is heartening to see
older men and women joining the young in
traditionally youth-oriented jobs such as in fast-
food restaurants and convenience stores.

Age is no barrier in areas of service to God.
Two million Hebrew slaves were rescued by an
80-year-old.
Isaac was born to a man who had already
passed his 100th birthday.
Anna the prophetess was 84 when she started
telling the world about Jesus.

Evelyn was a grieving widow whose husband
died just a few months before their dreams of
combined retirement were to come true. She was
convinced that her world died with him.
A year later she was using her late husband's
investments to send young men through seminary.
Later she paid her own expenses to the Philippines

where she spent three short but effective terms assisting career missionaries.

While speaking during Founder's Week at Moody Bible Institute, I met a young Filipino in training for ministry. He had been led to Christ during one of Evelyn's terms of service.

Barnie, the chief executive officer of a large northwest tool company, went to the Philippines with his wife after his retirement.

The veteran career missionary who met them was stunned when he heard this former executive say to him, "All I want to do while I am here is to be your servant."

Barnie and his wife served the missionaries faithfully. In addition, they established numerous home Bible study classes and led 50 Filipinos to Christ.

Kermit and Jean applied to teach in a missionary children's school in Africa after retirement from public school teaching. Despite the nagging pain of advanced arthritis, the couple served two terms and experienced the happiest and most productive years of their lives.

Wilbur and Floyd were retired executives. Both joined my pastoral staff as "dollar-a-year men" and performed invaluable ministries.

Chuck and Gladys stayed home after retirement and sent literally tons of supplies to overseas missionaries.

My mother is over 90 years old. Since she was widowed at 55, she has house-mothered more than seven hundred college students in Oregon. Today she rides the city bus to work daily. She serves as a foster grandparent.

Now that people are living longer and are more financially independent, the Church has the largest contingent of available people at her disposal of any time in her long history.

Retirement is no longer a prison, but an escape to areas of exciting and productive opportunity.

There are also some disadvantages to growing older.

My graying hair is a constant reminder that some changes are taking place.
I walk a little slower
  hear a little less
   and see with greater difficulty.
My muscles are shrinking.
My skin is wrinkling.
Reaction time is slowing.
My limbs are losing some of their strength and speed.
Body fat is harder to lose.
And my grandchildren are getting heavier.

In spite of the slowing of physical functions, it is encouraging to realize that only 5 percent of all senior citizens live in care facilities.

Only 15 percent are cared for by members of their families.

Of all the people over 65 years of age in this country, 80 percent are living independent lives and 82 percent are in moderate or good health.

You can grow old gracefully.

Good physical health is a necessity.

Essential health ingredients include
  a nutritious diet
    regular exercise
      adequate rest
        and periodic diversion
          from the stresses of life.
Dr. Ronald M. Lawrence, in his book *Going the Distance*, claims that it is always possible to improve our health. Men and women can actually get healthier as they grow older.

Physical fitness programs which include good nutrition and moderate exercise can enable people in their 70s to enjoy greater fitness and vigor than ever before.

An aerobic exercise like daily walking can facilitate in the aging the stamina and health of a much younger person. Regular exercise can cause a weight loss of as much as 18 pounds in a year.

Keep busy. Retirement can be deadly if it means the absence of work and goals.

Economic security is essential.

The Social Security Act of 1935 has been acclaimed the single most important event in American history for making economic independence available to the aging.

I began making contributions in 1940. At age 62 I can begin drawing from its benefits. If I choose to wait until I'm 65, my income will increase almost 25 percent.

At age 70, I can receive my Social Security payments plus an unlimited amount of earnings from wages.

Social Security is not enough. It does provide a limited amount of economic independence. But most working people have other retirement programs such as individual retirement accounts (IRA), pension plans, investment programs, annuities, and savings.

Medicare, plus a private health and hospital program, can eliminate the fear of the expense of a prolonged illness.

Inexpensive term insurance can provide for the inevitable funeral expenses that run on the average of three thousand dollars or more.

For even greater peace of mind, funeral arrangements should be discussed in advance.

Estate planning, including the preparation of a will, is a necessity.

It is this kind of financial planning that has permitted 80 percent of Americans to live independently after retirement.

The most important decision I ever made, one that has given serenity and meaning to the aging process, occurred when I was nine years old.

I received the Lord Jesus Christ as my personal Savior and experienced the love and forgiveness of God. I decided that life was too complex without God and that eternity was too frightening without forgiveness.

Since that moment I have lived with the assurance that whenever and however death comes, I will go to Heaven to spend eternity with Jesus Christ.

That all-important decision has not only given hope for the future. It has also removed much of the fear of the present.

God has made provisions for the present.

In Psalm 23 we are told that God has made ample provision for both our present and our future:

> "Surely goodness and lovingkindness
> will follow me all the days of my life,
> and I will dwell in the house of the
> LORD forever" (Psalm 23:6).

Heaven is God's provision for the future.

Goodness and lovingkindness are God's provision for the present.

God's goodness provides me with the good times in life—

> when the children are small
> the fire is warm
> the cupboard is full
> and the heart is at peace.

Times of goodness are when

> the body is strong
> funds are available
> and friends are near.

These are the times when the blessing of God is obvious and His presence is felt.

Lovingkindness is God's provision for the hard times in life—

> when health is failing

savings are depleted
and energies are low.

These are the times when circumstances loom
as tragedies and life is measured in terms of loss.

In these times God intervenes in mercy and
moves in to comfort an aching heart or strengthen
a tired body.

These divine twins, goodness and lovingkindness, are the Christian's ever-present
companions. They provide peace for the todays of
life and hope for our tomorrows.

Goodness and lovingkindness are God's special
provision for the 20 percent of our population
which does not enjoy good health or adequate
finances.

My grandmother was an overweight diabetic
who suffered from a diseased heart. She lived in a
small rented house which she was unable to
maintain. Her rent was paid from public funds.

I have never witnessed greater serenity than
what my grandmother displayed.

She treasured her Bible and her rocker.
She loved her family and lived in the expectancy of
Heaven. Goodness and lovingkindness sustained
her even when health had failed and wealth had
moved beyond her reach.

Aging begins at birth, continues through life,
and ceases at death. There are no aging people in
Heaven. The handicaps and limitations of physical
life will be laid aside. We will be given a new body
which, according to the promise of God, stays
forever young.

The Bible tells us:

> "For this perishable must put on the imperishable, and this mortal must put on immortality. But when this perishable will have put on the imperishable, and this mortal will have put on immortality, then will come about the saying that is written, 'Death is swallowed up in victory' " (1 Corinthians 15:53,54).

What a prospect!

What a future!

With that to look forward to, even growing older can be fun.

For Further Reading

Herbert DeVries. *Fitness After Fifty*. New York: Charles Scribner's Sons, 1987.

John Gillies. *A Guide to Caring For and Coping With the Aging Parents*. Nashville: Thomas Nelson Publishers, 1981.

Lanson Ross. *Total Life Prosperity*. Wheaton, IL: Tyndale House Publishers, 1971.

B. F. Skinner. *Enjoy Old Age*. New York: Warner Books, 1985.

Dying

❦

Is everyone afraid to die?

Why are we afraid to die?

*How can the fear of death be lessened
or eliminated?*

What actually happens when we die?

*Will anyone be spared
the experience of death?*

*What promises has God made which speak
to our fears?*

Lord, I've got a problem.
I don't want to die.
I know what the Bible says about Heaven,
but I still don't want to die. 🍎

Hezekiah was one of the good old kings. He lived while Isaiah was one of the good old prophets.

Good old kings and good old prophets were in short supply in the days of Judah.

Hezekiah met every crisis in Judah and defeated all of her enemies—even the Assyrians.

And then he was told that it was time for him to die.

He wept
he prayed

he bargained
   he pled with God
      for just a few more years.

He wrote an ode to God about death. You can read it in Isaiah 38:10-20.

He said all the things we'd like to say—if we would or could.

But he said them to God.

Hezekiah pondered: "Am I to die in the middle of my life?

Am I to be deprived of the rest of my years?

I won't see my friends or family again.

My body will be rolled up like a tent.

My life is going to end!

I'm bitter.

I don't want to die.

I want to live and give thanks, and tell my sons about You, and play my songs, and sing my praises.

O God, I can't give You thanks in the grave."

Hezekiah didn't want to die. He wanted to live and so do we.

My wife and I recently had one of those rare, cherished visits with her 93-year-old mother.

As we prepared to leave we noticed Mom's spirit begin to sag.

"Mom, you seem sad today," I said. Then I asked, "Is there anything we can do?"

"No," she answered. "I just don't want you to go."

"Why?" I pursued. "Are you afraid you might die before we see you again?"

"Yes," she admitted quickly. "I'm afraid I might not see you again."

Another family member spoke up. "Don't talk like that, Mother. You're not going to die."

"Yes she is," I interjected. "And it won't hurt her to talk about it."

We went on to address her fears. We planned another visit which was soon enough to give her peace and hope about the near future.

We don't want to die.
We don't like to talk about death.
And we certainly don't want to die now.

I recently visited with a dear friend who is witty, loving, godly, 85, and dying.

For more than 50 years she faithfully served alongside her pastor-husband, escorting people through life and preparing them for Heaven.

Now it was her turn.

She could find no relief from the pain of cancer that had ravaged every part of her body.

"Pastor, will you pray that the Lord will take me home?" she asked.

"Certainly," I answered. "When do you want to go—right now, tonight, or tomorrow?"

"Tomorrow," she answered with a slight twinkle in her pain-dulled eyes.

No one wants to die today.

Why are we so afraid of death?

God created us to live. He never planned death as a part of the human experience.

Man was mentally, emotionally, and spiritually programmed to live forever.

Adam and Eve could have lived without aging and dying if it had not been for their act of disobedience.

Death is an intruder.
Death is an enemy and we instinctively fear it.
Death is a great blow to our fragile egos.
To many, death is the ultimate failure.
Medical science boasts of lengthening the average life span to 70 years. Yet according to Psalm 90:10, man's life expectancy was 70 years more than three thousand years ago.

Will we ever eliminate the fear of death?

No, not completely.
We can block out the fear of death.
We can smother it with thoughts of living, but it will always surface again.
But as death approaches, God gives us dying grace. He calms our fears. He even provides us with peace.
He often causes His own even to welcome death.

How can we lessen our fear of death?

Accept your responses to death as normal.

Elizabeth Kubler-Ross, in her book *On Death and Dying*, identifies five emotions that are common to those who are approaching death.

They are
    denial
     anger
      bargaining
       depression
       and finally acceptance.

Did you notice the presence of all five responses in Hezekiah's ode? And Hezekiah's words were recorded twenty-seven hundred years before *On Death and Dying*.

Talk about death.

We don't need to overdo it, but occasionally it is good to include the subject of death in family discussions.

Use the word "death." Don't always substitute mysterious terms like "gone away" or "passed away."

Be prepared to tell the children about death. They usually accept death much more readily than adults.

I often look for acceptable ways to talk about death with the dying. The hardest part of the conversation is the opening.

I will ask patients: "Are you afraid?" It's surprising how often they will relax and discuss their feelings with me.

I often ask the critically ill: "Are you going to die?"

In most cases they already know. It is then possible to talk to them about death with meaning and purpose.

Facing death with silence often leaves profound regrets. A widower who could not handle talking about his wife's death was overwhelmed by one memory—"We didn't even get to say 'good-bye.' "

Jesus discussed His approaching death frankly and repeatedly:

> "Behold, we are going up to
> Jerusalem, and the Son of Man will be
> delivered up to the chief priests and
> the scribes; and they will condemn
> Him to death, and will deliver Him up
> to the Gentiles. And they will mock
> Him and spit upon Him, and scourge
> Him, and kill Him, and three days
> later He will rise again" (Mark
> 10:33,34).

That's a pretty grim scenario. But the disciples needed to be prepared for it.

Prepare for death.

My wife and I used to belong to a "Breakfast Club"—four couples who met for breakfast once a month.

At one of our meetings we discussed the subject of death. We clumsily asked each other some questions about death:

What would you do if your spouse died?
What funeral home would you call?
What sort of funeral would you have?
Who would preach the funeral sermon?
Where would you bury him or her?

To our mutual surprise, none of us had made these decisions.

After a long discussion we all agreed that we preferred a private burial service as early as possible.

Those of us who were eligible preferred to be buried in a veteran's cemetery.

If a memorial service was desired, it could be conducted at the church by the pastor for any who wished to attend.

The decisions we made that day didn't seem too significant to any of us—until one of our number died suddenly.

It was then that our sober breakfast discussion became important.

The questions had already been answered. The decisions had already been made.

The first question you will be asked after a loved one dies is, "What funeral home would you like us to call?"

The other questions we discussed at breakfast that day will also be posed.

Prepare for death by discussing these questions now and recording your decisions where they can easily be found.

Draw up a will.

Consider the Lord's work in your estate planning.

My wife and I have always given at least one-tenth of our income to the Lord's work. We are leaving at least that amount of our estate to the Lord.

Provide adequate insurance.

Burial expenses will range upward from five hundred dollars. An average funeral can easily cost three thousand dollars.

Receive God's gift of eternal life.
If you have never accepted the love and forgiveness of God, give this decision high priority in your life.

Keep forgiveness current.
I have seen families and friends subjected to a great deal of anguish because of death-bed confessions.

Learn about Heaven.

To dwell on the past makes dying increasingly difficult.
I asked my mother-in-law recently how she was dealing with the prospect of someday leaving her loved ones. She told me she was reading about Heaven every day.
As she directed her thoughts toward Heaven, she found that her fear was lessening and her desire to go there was increasing.

Learn what happens when we die.

Much of our fear of death stems from ignorance.
The apostle Paul responded to questions about death by saying:
"We do not want you to be uninformed, brethren, about those

who are asleep" (1 Thessalonians
4:13).
He then proceeded to tell them what will
actually happen to the dead and the living on the
day of resurrection.

Will anyone be spared the experience of death?

Certainly!
The Bible says that not everyone will die.
According to 1 Corinthians 15:51, one entire
generation of believers will avoid death.
This exciting prospect for the believer is called
"the rapture" or "the blessed hope."
The rapture is that moment in time when Jesus
will come to lift His Church out of the world and
transform us into spiritual beings apart from death.
Every Christian who ever lived has cherished
this hope.
Time has dulled this hope in many.
Today many feel that, because the rapture
hasn't happened, it won't happen.
But this generation of Christians just may be
the one which will not die.

Even with the comfort of the Scriptures we are
still afraid of death.
It's not death that we fear—it's dying.
I have a pretty good idea of what death is all
about, but I'm not sure just how or when it's going
to happen to me.
It's at this point that faith must take over.
Faith must plant itself firmly in the statements
God has made about dying.

God has already told us in our favorite Psalm:
"Even though I walk through the
valley of the shadow of death, I fear
no evil; for Thou art with me" (Psalm
23:4).
A valley is like a tunnel. It has an opening at both ends. Like a tunnel, death may be dark and frightening. But the experience is only temporary.

Death is only a shadow—"the shadow of death."
It is not a reality.
Shadows can frighten, but they can never hurt.
No one dies alone—"for Thou art with me."
God promises that we will not enter the inevitable, frightening experience of death alone. He will be with us.

You're still afraid?
So am I.
We will continue to do all in our power to remain alive. But when death finally comes, everything will be all right.
God knew how to take His own Son through the experience. He'll do the same for us.

Incidentally, in case you don't know the rest of the story of Hezekiah,
God answered his prayer
healed his body
and extended his life for
15 more years.
God knows how to heal too.

For Further Reading

Don Baker. *Heaven*. Portland, OR: Multnomah Press, 1986.

Elizabeth Kubler-Ross. *On Death and Dying*. New York: MacMillan Publishing Company, 1969.

Carl J. Scherzer. *Ministering to the Dying*. Philadelphia: Fortress Press, 1963.

Frustration

*Where can we turn
when we run out of options?*

*Is God really interested
in the little problems of my life?*

How can my prayers be effective?

Lord, I've got a problem.
My cursor is cussing at me. My computer
is stuck. I'm helpless. What can I do? 🍎

I was just finishing the 12th page of the chapter on dying.
The text was almost finished.
I had rewritten it 11 times.
As I stared at the monitor I was pleased with what I saw.
 The words were choice
   the layout was readable
    the thoughts were coherent
     and it was ready to be printed.

Then it happened.

Suddenly and with startling finality, right in the middle of a sentence, the computer stopped.

The screen was still illuminated

    the text was still readable

      but the cursor was gone.

At least the cursor wasn't where it belonged.

(The cursor is the little light that moves across the screen telling you exactly where you are working. It's a terribly important element of a computer. It's designed to respond to every command that comes through the keyboard.)

I found it hiding in the upper left corner of the screen, blinking its little green face at me.

My cursor would do nothing it was told to do.

I punched every one of my 82 keys, plus the space bar, once, twice, five times—nothing.

I held the keys down, but all I got was a high-pitched squeal, as if each punch of the keys brought pain to that infernal little cursor.

Nothing worked.

I couldn't type.

I couldn't print.

I couldn't save.

I called my son—an expert with computers—in Seattle.

His first question was, "Did you save any of the copy, Dad?"

"No," I answered.

"But Dad"—and he said it very respectfully—"you should stop typing every few paragraphs or pages and save your copy so you won't lose it if something goes wrong."

"I know, I know, Son, but I didn't."

He called a friend with IBM and explained my predicament. His friend's first question was, "Did he save any of the copy before it happened?"

When he heard that I hadn't, he suggested a combination of keystrokes—that didn't work.

Then he said, "I've had the same thing happen to me. The only way to correct the problem is to shut down the machine. When you turn it back on, everything should be all right."

"The only problem," I protested, "is that I'll lose hours and hours of completed writing."

"The thing to do," he responded, "is to get away from the machine—take a long walk. Accept the fact that you've lost your text. Then sit down and try to recall what you've written and write it again."

I screamed—softly.

I know grown men are not supposed to scream. But I screamed.

Going through the process of rewriting a finished chapter would be something like a mother giving birth to the same baby twice.

I called Kathy Rausch of the IBM computer training school in Portland.

She understood the problem immediately.

Her first question was, "Did you save any of the copy."

"No, I didn't save any of the copy."

•

"You probably ought to stop every . . ."

"I know," I said.

"You'll probably have to switch it off to correct it."

There it was again. The only possible solution to my problem was to switch off the machine and lose an entire chapter—with my deadline just three days away.

I knew that the moment I switched the "off" button the words would disappear forever.

"By the way," Kathy asked, "what are you writing?"

"A book," I replied.

"What's the title?"

"Lord, I've Got a Problem."

I thought she would never stop laughing.

"I love it, I love it," she said. "I hope you include a chapter about your cursor. You really *do* have a problem."

I don't know how many times I continued to punch the keys with that obstinate little cursor screaming back at me.

It took on a personality.

It became a rebellious little child who refused to obey my commands.

Then it became the Devil.

I finally
  gave up
   left the machine running
    went for a long walk
     recalled what I could

jotted down some notes
and reached for the "off" button.

Suddenly, I remembered that I had another
option.

Resigned to my loss, but willing to try
anything, I bowed my head over the computer and
prayed.

"Father," I said, "I really don't have time to do
this chapter over again. You're the only possible
solution to my problem.

Please nudge my cursor back where it belongs.

Please free up the jammed mechanism.

Please repair this computer for me. I promise I
will save the copy from now on.

Please."

I must have sounded to God like King
Hezekiah as he was begging God to spare his life.

Within a few moments, without a sound,
the little cursor obeyed
the keyboard functioned
the computer worked
and my chapter was rescued.

I immediately saved all my previous work in
the chapter.

Then I stopped to thank God before I
continued to write.

When all else fails, pray.

Better yet, before all else fails, pray.

Jesus told a delightful little story in Luke
11:5-13.

An unnamed man was surprised by
unexpected company in the middle of the night.
His visitors were hungry and his bread box was
empty.

He went next door and pounded on his
neighbor's door asking for three loaves of bread to
feed his guests.

The neighbor, who had been asleep, was upset
at the disturbance and refused the request for food.

The host persisted. He pounded loud and long
until his neighbor finally
    dragged himself out of bed
     went downstairs
      opened the door
      and gave him the bread.
Jesus summarized the story by saying:
    "Even though he will not get up and
    give him anything because he is his
    friend, yet because of his persistence
    he will get up and give him as much
    as he needs" (Luke 11:8).

This story embodies one of our Lord's lessons
on prayer.

It teaches us three things about prayer.

First, God's level of interest includes everything.

There are no concerns in life which are beyond
the concern of God. Bread and cursors are as
important to God as life and death.

Second, prayer, to be effective, must be specific.

Three loaves were asked for—not "some," not "several." The harried host had determined his need carefully and then specified that need in his request.

Third, prayer, to be effective, must sometimes be persistent.

The neighbor in the story got up and gave, not because of friendship, but because of the man's persistence. Persistence is one way of demonstrating to God that our need is genuine and that our concern is real.
Jesus concluded the story with the words:
"Ask, and it shall be given to you;
seek, and you shall find; knock, and it
shall be opened to you" (Luke 11:9).

God delights in becoming involved with our problems like a man delights in being asked to do something for his wife.
Something good happens to my ego when my wife asks me to open a pickle jar.
Nothing can keep me from twisting that lid open, even if it means breaking it.
Handing that opened pickle jar back to my wife is a source of joy for me.
I did something for her that she asked me to do.
I did something for her that she couldn't do herself.

God's delight is just as real and satisfying as ours.

He loves to provide bread, repair computers and even open pickle jars. He loves it when, in our helplessness, we give Him our impossible problems. He loves to solve our problems because He loves us.

> "And everything you ask in prayer, believing, you shall receive" (Matthew 21:22).

For Further Reading

John Bisagno. *The Power of Positive Praying*. Grand Rapids, MI: Zondervan Publishing Company, 1985.

Manford G. Gutzke. *Plain Talk on Prayer*. Grand Rapids, MI: Baker, 1973.

Rosalind Rinker. *Prayer, Conversing with God*. Grand Rapids, MI: Zondervan Publishing Company.

Other Good
Harvest House Reading

PRIVATE PAIN
by *Rich Wilkerson*

Rich Wilkerson tells us that "Few are exempt from some degree of private pain"—emotional isolation, a sense of rejection, guilt, loneliness, depression. A powerful book that offers help and understanding.

OVERCOMING HURTS AND ANGER
by *Dr. Dwight Carlson*

Dr. Carlson shows us how to confront our feelings and negative emotions in order to experience liberation and fulfillment.

LIFE-CHANGING ANSWERS TO DEPRESSION
by *Harold Ivan Smith*
Through biblical insights, we are enabled to recognize and understand depression—and given practical helps to turn depression around.

GROWING THROUGH DIVORCE
by *Jim Smoke*

A practical guide for anyone facing divorce. This book can transform your life from an old ending to a new beginning and help to heal the deep hurts and doubts of anyone trapped in the despair of divorce.

STORMIE
by *Stormie Omartian*

The childhood of singer/songwriter Stormie Omartian was marred by physical and emotional abuse. Searching for an end to the inner turmoil which constantly confronted her in later years, Stormie found herself on the verge of suicide. This poignant story shows how God can bring help and hope to anyone who doubts the value of his or her own life.

Dear Reader:

We would appreciate hearing from you regarding this Harvest House nonfiction book. It will enable us to continue to give you the best in Christian publishing.

1. What most influenced you to purchase *Lord, I've Got a Problem?*
   - ☐ Author
   - ☐ Subject matter
   - ☐ Backcover copy
   - ☐ Recommendations
   - ☐ Cover/Title
   - ☐ _____

2. Where did you purchase this book?
   - ☐ Christian bookstore
   - ☐ General bookstore
   - ☐ Other
   - ☐ Grocery store
   - ☐ Department store

3. Your overall rating of this book:
   ☐ Excellent ☐ Very good ☐ Good ☐ Fair ☐ Poor

4. How likely would you be to purchase other books by this author?
   - ☐ Very likely
   - ☐ Somewhat likely
   - ☐ Not very likely
   - ☐ Not at all

5. What types of books most interest you?
   (check all that apply)
   - ☐ Women's Books
   - ☐ Marriage Books
   - ☐ Current Issues
   - ☐ Self Help/Psychology
   - ☐ Bible Studies
   - ☐ Fiction
   - ☐ Biographies
   - ☐ Children's Books
   - ☐ Youth Books
   - ☐ Other _____

6. Please check the box next to your age group.
   - ☐ Under 18
   - ☐ 18-24
   - ☐ 25-34
   - ☐ 35-44
   - ☐ 45-54
   - ☐ 55 and over

Mail to: Editorial Director
Harvest House Publishers
1075 Arrowsmith
Eugene, OR 97402

Name _____

Address _____

City _____ State _____ Zip _____

Thank you for helping us to help you in future publications!